LESSONS FOR OUR YOUNGER BROTHERS

Joseph Grisko

&

Jack Delehey

To our brothers, Jack and Tucker. This book is for you.

DEAR JACK,

I want to start off by saying that I love you and value our relationship more than you'll ever know. I've always admired your kind heartedness and selflessness and try to emulate these qualities in my own life. As your older brother, I feel privileged to have had the opportunity to learn from you and teach you lessons as we navigate life together.

When I reflect on my life, the time when I felt the least prepared were the few years post-college. At the time, I felt ready to enter the "real world", but in reality had no idea how to be an adult. Up until this point, I'd never done my taxes, had no idea how ask a girl on a real date, and couldn't cook anything outside of pasta.

My motivation for writing this book is to provide you guidance as you tackle life's hardest transition. I have learned a lot of lessons the hard way (see the chapter about when I purchased $68 of mac n cheese... yikes) and want to make sure you learn from my mistakes. As confident as I am that you will succeed on your own, my job as your older brother is to make life easier for you.

As you dive in, please read this book with an open mind. Some chapters are serious and teach you how to appreciate life; while others give you tips on how to throw a killer party (whichever is more important is for you to decide). By no means do I expect you to take all the advice I give, but if you learn one thing from this book and do something better than I did, I will feel like I accomplished my goal.

I am proud of the man you've become and look forward to seeing all that you achieve in the future. I want you to know that I am with you 150% in anything that you do, and feel honored to call you my brother.

Love,
Joey

DEAR TUCKER,

You may be six years younger than I but I want you to know just how much I look up to you. You constantly impress me with your imagination, work ethic, and passionate displays of creativity (I mean who else picks up a guitar and starts cranking out John Mayer songs flawlessly in a few weeks? Or rips up the piano in front of hundreds of people at Faneuil Hall...as a 12 year old? Or turns duct-tape wallets into a profitable business in middle school?)

The point is, Tuck, you are going places. With or without me you are going places in this world. And as crazy as it is, you'll be in the "real world" in a little more than a year. Crazy because it seems like just yesterday we moved you into your college dorm...

Move In Day. Tulane University. August 2016.

And while I am 100% certain you will thrive with or without my guidance, at the end of the day, I am your older brother. And as an older brother, if I can make one single thing even a little bit easier for you as you enter the next stage of your life, then I've done my job.

And that, right there, is the entire purpose of this book.

I am here to give you the advice Mom and Dad can't...and your peers simply don't know. Advice I have gained all on my own...from living and failing and (sometimes) succeeding.

It wasn't too long ago I graduated from college myself, which means one thing: I've learned a lot about the "real world" in a pretty short amount of time. I've made a ton of mistakes and luckily stumbled into a few successes as well. And while I think a crucial component of transitioning to adulthood *is* experiencing these challenges on your own, I also think not having to forge a completely new path each and every day might just make things a little easier for you.

100% of the chapters in this book come from our real-world experiences. None of it comes from any productivity gurus or life experts (although I had to get a couple of Cal Newport, Tim Ferriss quotes in there of course). Every chapter is based on an accumulation of tips and insights we've gained since we, ourselves, graduated from college in 2014. And while I certainly don't expect you to adopt every piece of advice (or even the majority), if you are able to adopt even just one single piece of advice then, like I said, I've done my job as an older brother in helping kickstart your transition after college.

I love you, Tuck. Congratulations on all your current success and cheers to all the future successes I know are bound to come. I am truly thankful to call you my brother.

Love,
Jack

CONTENTS

INTRODUCTION

WRITTEN BY KEVIN DELEHEY

Dear Reader,

Congratulations! Whether you are a young adult between the ages of eighteen and twenty-five or just an individual seeking self improvement, you have taken the first step to making your life significantly easier. In the pages that follow are life lessons, words of wisdom and practical advice for anyone entering their adult life or looking for daily practical advice.

In this book you will find everything from quick practical tips (such as morning routine hacks) to more insightful advice on how to appreciate life and those around you. It is a por-pouri of life hacks that were learned the hard way...by the authors themselves...so you don't have to.

How do I know the pages that follow have merit? Simple. I am Jack's brother and lived with Joey and Jack for over a year. Let me re-phrase that: Jack and Joey let me crash on their couch when I first moved to Denver and I had no place to stay. Now I've upgraded from the couch and am their roommate. I'll admit it: they don't just talk the talk, they walk the walk. They live and utilize these tips to follow in their daily lives. I've seen it firsthand.

Jack and Joey have been fantastic role models for me to follow. Not only did they give me a home when I was in need, but even more importantly they have been two strong role models who have guided me on how to behave as a young adult. Their generosity, positivity, thoughtfulness and ambition gave me a model on which to base my behavior.

Unlike most of you picking up this book, I did not have to read their book to learn their lessons. I saw them make the world a better place to those around them every day and learned from experience.

Early adult life can be difficult, scary, trying, and most of all confusing. Fortunately, we all don't need to make the same mistakes to learn the same lessons. Jack and Joey have done that for you so you don't have to learn these lessons the hard way.

So congratulations. Your life is about to get a heck of a lot easier.

-Kevin Delehey
(Brother, Roommate, and Friend)

GOING ON REAL DATES IS A THING NOW

How To Crush First Dates

L et's be honest, up until this point in your life chances are you've never been on a real first date. Bringing your high school girlfriend to The Melting Pot with your parent's credit card doesn't count. And taking some girl you met at 2 AM to a fraternity date party certainly doesn't count either.

A real first date is when you ask someone you hardly know to spend 3 hours making small talk while doing an activity that you had to plan. The woman will likely judge you off the itinerary and "vibe" of the date (whether she realizes it or not). If you don't nail it, chances are you won't land that coveted second date. Women expect these dates to be original, fun, and telling of who you are as a person. Let's focus on these three pillars to ensure you crush the first date.

BE ORIGINAL

If your itinerary is not at least somewhat original, your date will likely assume you are like every other guy that didn't work out and could write you off from the start. We have a girlfriend in Chicago that coined the term "Playbook" to classify these dates. A "Playbook" date is one that a guy runs over and over again with different women because it requires zero creative effort and has possibly been successful in the past. Think of it like running "The Option" in football; it's a bread and butter play that every team runs because it's led to touchdowns in the past, but at this point the defense is ready for it and knows how to stop it.

Our girlfriend described a "Playbook" date going something like this: date starts at a hole in the wall mom and pop Italian place, then to a bar to shoot pool and play darts, and finally end at an ice cream shop to split a sundae. Our friend claims she's been on the exact same date 5 different times with 5 different guys while in Chicago. Unsurprisingly, she never dated any of these guys long term.

My advice to you when planning a date is to get creative and pick an activity that you actually enjoy doing. If you hate arcade games, don't bring a girl to an arcade bar. She will tell right away that you're not having fun and will assume it is a result something that she's doing. Picking an activity that you like will make you more relaxed and come off more confident to the woman. Being creative will separate you from the pack, make your date memorable, and will put you in a much better position to land a second date.

MAKE IT FUN

Movies are the worst date idea ever. *Whoever deemed the dinner/movie combo as being a fun first date single handedly tarnished billions of potential relationships.* Not only are movies unoriginal, but you can't talk so each person leaves the date not knowing anything about the other person. After reflecting on the date, the woman will most likely not have a favorable taste in her mouth--a text for date #2 is unlikely.

I have found the most successful dates are ones that are active and allows you both to accomplish something together. A good example of this is rock climbing. Rock climbing is the perfect first date because it is scary to someone unfamiliar with the sport, and everyone can reach the clearly defined goal (getting to the top of the wall) with a little effort. Conversations during these dates are often light and effortless and the woman leaves feeling like you helped her achieve something she originally thought was unattainable. And if a woman doesn't like rock climbing (or at least isn't willing to give it a try), she might not be a good match for you in the first place.

Another trick of the pros to making a date fun is to change locations throughout the date. Changing physical locations breaks the date up into phases and makes it seem like you guys did a lot together even though you'll spend the same amount of time as a three hour dinner. I typically use Google Maps beforehand to make sure I pick places that are walkable to each other. During the transition phase from one place to another is a prime time to make a move for a kiss (you'll likely be more successful than waiting until the very end when the kiss/no kiss decision can get awkward).

BE TELLING OF WHO YOU ARE

The overall goal of the date is for you both to determine if you like each other enough to merit a second date. If you leave the date not knowing much about the other person, both of you probably won't want to pursue date number two.

My advice is to make a sincere effort to be yourself. I know this sounds cliche and matter of fact, but I can't tell you how many times I've been on dates and tried to tailor my actions to what I think the woman would like as opposed to being myself. Not only is it more difficult to be someone you're not, but the goal is for the woman to like you for being you, not someone you made up.

So going with this theme, when picking an activity, find something that is important to you. If you're a hockey player, take her to a hockey game. If you love nerdy board games, take her to a nerdy board game bar (shout out Settlers of Catan). If you're into live Jazz music, take her to a Jazz show. *A date that aligns with what you enjoy will show the woman that you are passionate about something and will allow for more fluid conversations.*

You're better than the cheesy overdone first date. You got this.

WE RECOMMEND NOT BUYING $68 OF MAC N CHEESE

... And Other Financial Advice

Y ou have money now, congratulations! I remember getting my first real job pay check and thinking, "Wow, that's a shit ton of money." This chapter is all about how to make that paycheck go further. But first let's start with a story...

It was November 2014 and I was invited to my first Friendsgiving in Chicago. For those that are unfamiliar, a Friendsgiving is when a group of friends coordinate a Thanksgiving dinner (usually before the holiday itself) and everyone is expected to bring their favorite Thanksgiving dish. Being fresh out of college and not knowing how to cook, I immediately volunteered to make mac n cheese. I mean I knew how to make pasta with marinara, how much different could mac n cheese be?

Friendsgiving day rolls around and naturally I procrastinate in preparing my mac. While my friends were spending hours baking a turkey, I was rolling out of bed at noon with a massive headache from the night before. Instead of doing the logical thing and immediately going to the grocery store to get ingredients and begin cooking, I decided it'd be easier to pick up premade mac n cheese from Whole Foods on my way. My logic was it'd be better than anything I could toss together and would save me tons of hungover effort. Seemed like a no brainer.

After scooping out what I estimated to be enough mac n cheese for ten people and giving it to the supermarket attendant, I was confident I made the right decision. Until I saw the price... $68! For mac n cheese. I couldn't believe it. I could've made it for ¼ the price. At this point there was no turning back. I unwillingly paid the attendant and went on my way.

I later found out that all Whole Foods hot bar items were priced by weight, and mac n cheese isn't necessarily the lightest item. My Whole Foods blunder was my first of many experiences ineffectively spending my money. To avoid doing stupid shit with your money like I did, here are a few financial tips:

ESTABLISH CREDIT EARLY

Now that you're old you have this thing called a credit score. The earlier you start establishing credit, the higher this score will be. Build your credit as soon as possible by opening up a credit card. Even if you are fresh out of college you can most likely get a credit card from the bank that hosts your account and provides your debit card. *Having a good credit score is important because you will receive lower interest rates when borrowing from a bank.* You'll be buying a wedding ring or house before you know it. Additionally, and perhaps more important for your immediate future, *nearly every apartment application will complete a background check that includes checking your credit score.* Build up your credit and you'll breeze through these applications.

MAX OUT YOUR 401K

If you talk to any financial advisor he will tell you the smartest way to save for retirement is to start young. The earlier you start, the more you can compound your savings for when you need it the most. *If your company offers a 401k match program, at a bare minimum contribute the maximum amount your company will match. This is free money.*

OPEN A ROTH IRA, 401K, OR BOTH

Roth IRAs and Roth 401ks are two of best tools to save money. *They allow you to invest money and get taxed today, opposed to when you decide to take your money out.* The reason this is so great is because you will likely be making more money at 63 opposed to at 23 so you will be taxed in a lower bracket.

SAVE, SAVE, SAVE

If you can't tell already, I want you to save. The old saying "A dollar saved is a dollar earned" is completely wrong. *A dollar saved is actually worth significantly more than a dollar earned.* The reason is twofold:

- *Taxes:* Every dollar you saved has already been taxed, while future money to-be-earned still needs to be taxed. So if you "earn" one dollar more, this is truly more like 88 cents after taxes (depending on your tax bracket it could be less, actually). On the other hand if you already have a dollar in your back account, that means the dollar has already been taxed and is therefore more valuable than a dollar that has yet to be earned!

- *Time Value of Money:* The second reason saving is worth more than earning is because you can invest your savings and earn a return. Think of it like making money while you sleep. If you invest $1,000 and make a 10% return (granted, a very nice return but hey, it's for the example), at the end of the year you will have made $100 for doing literally nothing. Pretty cool, huh?

BUY RENTERS INSURANCE

Renters insurance is God's gift to carefree 22 year olds. Imagine losing your $2,500 watch at bar at 3AM. Or getting $4,000 worth of laptops stolen out of your rental car. Or locking a $2,700 generator to a fence only to have it get stolen in a matter of hours (bizarre story, best be left untold). Or having not one but two cars broken into...These are all hypotheticals of course... But seriously, a common misconception is renters insurance only covers items stolen, damaged, or broken that are physically in your home (or apartment). This is not true. It will cover your personal items that are outside your home as well. Typically $150 to $250 dollars per year covers you up to $25,000 or $30,000. We have made probably 4 or 5 insurance claims since being out of college and it has saved us thousands of dollars.

PLAY THE CREDIT CARD GAME

Credit card companies will give you hundreds of dollars of value to sign up for their credit card. I have flown to Spain and Hawaii for free just for signing up for a card during one of these promotions. These cards often require you to spend a certain amount of money over a course of 3 to 4 months to earn the bonus (it's usually something along the lines of "spend $3,000 in the first 3 months to earn 50,000 points"). I recommend monitoring these sign up bonuses and taking advantage of them. I am constantly opening and closing credit cards (aka credit card churning) to game the system to pay for my next vacation. It's a misconception that card churning lowers your credit score. In reality it actually improves your score because having multiple cards means you are spending significantly less than your available credit, a characteristic that is viewed positively in the eyes of credit bureaus.

TGIW

The saying TGIF or 'Thank God It's Friday' is so popular in American culture that there's a chain of 870 restaurants named after this expression. I can guarantee at least once a week a colleague of mine will start an email or call with "Happy Friday!" I am guilty of this myself, however, *why does it need to be Friday to be a happy day? Why can't it be "Thank God It's Wednesday"?*

Years ago I pondered these questions when I realized I was living my whole life for the weekend. Monday through Friday afternoon was work, Friday night was when I came alive again, Saturday was always the best day of my week, Sunday morning was recovery, and Sunday night was spent preparing for Monday. On any given week I would only enjoy 2 out of the 7 days. *I was essentially throwing 5/7th of my life away.* This was not cutting it for me.

My whole life turned around when Saturday wasn't consistently the best day of my week. I started implementing things like #MakeMondayGreatAgain or #TreatYourselfTuesday to help enjoy the days I used to dread. Yes, it is obviously much harder when work takes up a minimum of 8 hours out of your weekdays, however, I found that little things before or after work can save these precious days. Here are a few examples of weekday savers:

- Spontaneously buy yourself a gift.
- Ask a random friend, girlfriend, or maybe-someday-girlfriend out to a trendy new restaurant you've always wanted to go to.
- Find a bar that specializes in a random weekday and tear it up (if you're ever in Chicago on a Thursday night, go to Durkin's for $3 pitchers. You won't regret it).

- Change up your workout routine and do something badass. For example, instead of doing the same boring old running route, get in your car, drive to the beach, and crush some sprints in the sand.
- Join an intramural league that holds games on a weekday night. It can be a super intense men's league or a relaxed co-ed league that goes out for beers afterwards. Two different vibes but each accomplish the same goal: keeping the weekdays exciting.

You get the point. It doesn't have to be the weekend for you to enjoy your life and you don't have to travel to go on vacation. Take advantage of what's in your backyard. Explore your home city on a weekday and do something that will make you think... Thank God It's Wednesday!

DO SOMETHING UNCOMFORTABLE ONCE A WEEK

From October 11, 2015 to October 11, 2016, I did a year long experiment with two friends (one of which was Jack, the other co-author of this book) that changed my life forever. Before I get into what we did, and what you can do to live a more fulfilling life, let's start with a quote:

You never change your life until you step out of your comfort zone; change begins at the end of your comfort zone - Roy T. Bennett

---

ORIGIN OF *UNCOMFORTABLE MATRIX* (AS TOLD BY JOEY)

The idea started with an epiphany. I spent years pondering why I was much happier abroad in Africa (where I studied in Spring 2013) than at home with my family and friends. I came to realize that it wasn't the place that made me happy, but my mindset while there. While in Africa, I was constantly challenged by everyday life, questioning lifelong beliefs after being surrounded by extreme poverty, and learning from people with backgrounds drastically different from my own. In short, Africa forced me outside my comfort zone in the most extreme ways possible. I knew if I wanted to grow at home as I did in Africa, I needed to find ways to challenge myself in my everyday life.

That is where the idea for the *Uncomfortable Matrix* came from. Jack, our friend Sam, and I decided we were going to do one uncomfortable activity a week for an entire year and document the results in an Excel spreadsheet. It could be something as small as buying an overly trendy piece of clothing, or as large as deciding to move across the country. If someone didn't complete an uncomfortable task that week, they were forced to pay $5 into a jar that we kept in our kitchen. The beauty of the jar was it was based on a honor code. Something might be uncomfortable for one person, but not another. The whole point of the exercise was to grow as people, not to one up each other by doing more and more absurd shit.

At the end of the year, the three of us printed out the *Uncomfortable Matrix*, tossed on some blazers, and used the money we collected on a steak dinner. The dinner probably lasted three hours, as we went line by line reflecting on how much we grew over the past year. Here is a screenshot of a portion of the matrix to provide some context:

Week Ending	Complete (Brief Description of Event)			Incomplete (Pay $5 Fine)		
	Joey	Del	Shwab	Joey	Del	Shwab
10/11/2015	Went to hot yoga for first time	Went to church (in dallas)		I got uncomfortable	I got uncomfortable	Paid
10/18/2015	Bought trendy pants / asked out co-worker (Ashwini)	Conversation with a sweet, old, crippled lady at the gym - her name is Susan, she is a sweetheart	Solo yoga w/ armpit hair lady	I got uncomfortable	I got uncomfortable	I got uncomfortable
10/25/2015	Stayed with Mr. Krebs in Nashville w/o Krebs		Told (not asked) my boss that I would not come in to work on Wednesday	I got uncomfortable	Paid	I got uncomfortable
11/1/2015	Conversation with homeless man in San Francisco park	Swam laps, almost fainted		I got uncomfortable	I got uncomfortable	Paid

WHY IS IT IMPORTANT TO GET UNCOMFORTABLE? (AS TOLD BY JACK)

What the *Uncomfortable Matrix* taught the three of us is just how powerful your mind is. *Uncomfortable*, at the end of the day, is just a feeling that's in your head! And realizing this through repeated, methodical trial truly changed our lives for the better. It made us realize just how many of our goals could be accomplished by simply getting into a different mental state and overcoming fears. Once the *Uncomfortable Matrix* got rolling, I saw it translating to other parts of life: more confidence proposing unique solutions at work, more confidence approaching females at the bar or gym, more confidence trying new different things, whether it be food or workout classes or anything else. "What's the worst that can happen?" became a constant question to myself and the answer was almost always the same-- the *worst case scenario* really just wasn't that bad at all. So your boss rejects your idea--so what? So that girl at the bar tells you she has a boyfriend and walks away-- so what? Once you get in this mental state, it's a damn powerful feeling.

We started with a quote, so let's end with one:

A person's success in life can usually be measured by the number of uncomfortable conversations he or she is willing to have. - Tim Ferriss

---

This conversation can be with someone else or, as it was with us, it can be with *yourself, in your head.* We've seen it first-hand--the more you are willing to have that uncomfortable conversation with yourself, and then push forward with the obstacle at hand, the more fulfilled you'll be. Writing this book is a prime example. You know what else is? Going on a Grouper date with three random strangers...we did that too...but that's a story for another time.

"IT ALL COMES OUT IN THE WASH" ... EXCEPT IT DOESN'T AT ALL... BUT THAT'S OKAY

You ever hear the phrase, "It all comes out in the wash"? Yep we have too...and did for years. Let us tell you something:

That phrase is total bs...and that's okay. The truth is, it doesn't all come out in the wash. Someone will always end up fronting more than their fair share. Believe us, it's much, much better to be on the giving side of the equation than receiving side.

In short, this chapter could probably be titled "How Not To Be a Mooch." But at closer examination, it's more than that. It's a chapter about including others, demonstrating a willingness to be the leader & organizer (for more on that, see the chapter "If You Build It, They Will Come") and how to make everyone in the room feel like the most important person. And yes, if you want to do all these things, it may end up with you coming out on the negative side of the financial situation...but we're here to tell you that's okay. And in fact, you should embrace it. *Because what you lose in $ you'll make up tenfold in memories, stories, lifelong connections, and people who are willing to go above and beyond for you at a later date.*

Situations in which no one has ever actually broken even in the history of mankind:
  1. **Hosting a Party**

2. **Restaurant Tab:** "Hey guys, I'll pick up the bill, you all just Venmo me."
   (Note: no one ever adds tax & tip, ever.) (Second note: at least one person's
   Venmo "isn't working right now but I'll Venmo when it is.")

3. **Splitting Ubers:** If you ever have an Uber where everyone in the Uber
   actually successfully accepts the split, please email us immediately so we
   can worship you. We've never seen it happen...

We could go on and on. You get the picture. When you host, when you organize,
when you lead, *you will lose money*. Own it, embrace it, enjoy it. You want to be the
guys who hosts a party and, when that friend-of-a-friend arrives whom you don't
know, you slap a beer in his hand as he walks through the door. The beer cost you 75
cents you won't get back...and for the rest of time that dude will remember your
hospitality, feel welcome at your place, and feel like he can reach out to you when in
need. That's worth it. Every. Single. Time.

And on the other side of things, when you get invited to an event, don't be "that
guy" who shows up empty handed. Instead, be the guy that shows up with a 24-pack
that you leave behind as a thank you. It's a small price to pay financially and people
do notice. Be a giver, not a taker.

IF YOU DON'T MOVE TO CHICAGO AFTER COLLEGE YOU ARE WRONG

Just kidding. But in all seriousness, it is important to move to a new city at least once while you are still young enough to enjoy it. The friends you will meet and the experiences you will have will last a lifetime.

If you are trying to make friends in a new city, join an intramural sports team. Work friends are great, but it's important to have a break from the office on the weekends.

CALENDAR IS KEY

I n college, your life is pretty much mapped out for you. You show up on campus at the beginning of the semester, and are given a class schedule. If you're a good student, you go to most classes, if you're a bad student you probably don't. Either way, your calendar is dictated by the school. When you aren't in class, there are pretty much four things you're doing:

- Studying
- Partying
- Sleeping
- Eating

That's pretty much it. There really is very little need for a calendar because there just aren't that many things you could be doing at any one time. Even big things like vacations are usually planned for you. "Oh, looks like I just finished finals...Hey Mom, when is my flight home?"

All of that changes in the real world. If you don't have a sound system to keep track of appointments, tasks, to-do's, events etc, you will quickly find you are completely unprepared for the bombardment of such events. You will forget *a lot* of things. You will make lists and feel great about them...only to lose said list an hour later. Sometimes this will mess up your own life, which is manageable. But when it starts to mess up others' lives (aka your boss), you'll want to very quickly turn to this chapter and read below.

When you graduate from college, a calendar is absolutely *key* to crushing it in work and life. So before you groan, close this book, and go back to your FIFA game, here's a system that takes *no more than five minutes per day* and, I promise, will save you tremendous amounts of time in the long run.

THE 3-STEP, 5-MINUTE PER DAY CALENDAR PROCESS

Your work calendar, personal calendar, and anything-else-you-can-think-of calendar should all be *the same calendar*. Google Calendar or Outlook are the two best options. Productivity gurus love to make this complicated. And it's just completely unnecessary.

1. **Throughout your day, have a way to write down tasks immediately as they pop into your head.** Then forget about them...we'll come back to these later. This can be as simple as a piece of paper & pen in your pocket. But let's be honest, it's not 2004 anymore. Everyone has a smartphone. I recommend using the "Lists" app on the iPhone or even the notepad. If you feel like going extra fancy, there are a million task-tracking apps in the App Store as well.

2. **MOST IMPORTANT STEP – At the end of your day, go back to your list.** Before you go to bed, take out your list and review. Now move those items to your calendar. This is the step that people don't do and it's absolutely critical. Typical questions regarding this step:

   o "But I just don't know when I can get that task done!" - I don't care. You shouldn't care either. The fact that you have it on your list means you *want to get it done at some point*. So take your best guess at when you can get this task done (even if it is 3 months from now!) and get it on the calendar!

   o "I know what day I can get the task done, but have no idea what hour of the day I can fit it in to my schedule." - Utilize the all-day chunks at the top of the calendar and don't even think about what hour of the day you can fit them in until the night before. Below is a screenshot of my calendar for an upcoming day. Notice the use of "All-Day" events at the top (events that, at the moment, I don't know when I can complete). Also notice scheduled events down below (events that have a specific time slot already).

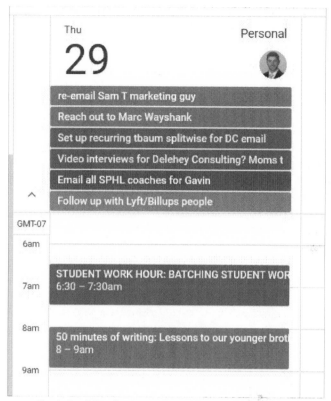

Jack's Calendar. "All-Day" tasks are up top and have yet to be assigned a time slot.

3. **Bill Belichick: "We're on to Cincinnati." / Jack Delehey & Joey Grisko: "We're on to tomorrow."** Once you've moved all tasks from your list and placed them on your calendar for some day in the future, now take a look at your calendar for tomorrow...and only tomorrow. Just like Bill Belichick focuses on one game at a time, you should focus on one day at a time. You will likely have several tasks that are listed as "All-Day" tasks. Now it's time to actually think about when, tomorrow, you can fit these tasks in! Another frequent question:

   o "I thought I could to it tomorrow but I just don't think I can fit it in..." - No problem, move the task to another day in the future. This will happen often. But here's the great part--once a task is in your calendar, there really is only one way for the task to *eventually* get off the calendar--for you to complete it!

PRO TIP - UTILIZE PRIVATE/ FREE SETTINGS

Whether using Google Calendar, Outlook, or something else, it is very easy to mark certain events (or even certain sub-calendars, ex: "Personal) completely private. So if you have a mid-day root canal and wouldn't like your entire office to know, simply mark as "Private"

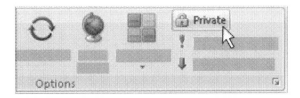

You also can mark calendar events as "Free." For example, let's say you have free time in the middle of the work day and want to pencil-in a phone call to your brother (aka me!) just to catch up. You could mark that event as "Free" (instead of the typical "Busy"). Therefore, if your boss does need to book that time on your calendar, it will show up as free and can be booked over. This is a really helpful trick when balancing personal events during working hours.

* * *

The key, like many suggestions in this book, is to make this 5-minute calendar process a nightly habit. The good news is, once you enter the real world and the commitments and tasks start piling up, you'll be forced, in a way, to find a system.

So instead of following the complicated and time-intensive advice from productivity gurus who have a wife, two kids, and haven't been out to a bar past 10pm in over a decade, follow our advice.

5 minutes a day keeps tomorrow's scaries away. Calendar is key.

IF YOUR COLLEGE FRIENDS DON'T HAVE A REUNION AT LEAST ONCE A YEAR YOU BETTER PLAN IT

F riendships fade fast when you no longer live right down the hall from each other. If you're like us, your college friends are some of your best friends in the world. Don't let these people out of your life.

Plan a trip once a year even when everyone says they are busy. If you do it the same weekend every year (Memorial Day, Labor Day, etc) your friends will mark it down on their calendars and will be more likely to attend. People will start getting married and having babies before you know it. Get the tradition started shortly after you graduate...and keep it going yearly as a guaranteed way to check in with your friends who are now likely scattered all across the country.

Vanderbilt Reunion: August 2016. Jack (lower left), Joey (3rd from top left)

20-4-1: THE THEORY TO LOCKING DOWN YOUR DREAM JOB (GIRL)

What if I told you that flirting with girls and applying for your dream job were similar. Would you believe me? One could argue which requires more skill, but what can't be argued is that *success is directly correlated to how comfortable you are with failure.* Let me explain.

20-4-1 stands for 20 approaches leads to 4 opportunities which results in 1 success. You can apply this theory to many aspects of life, as we've seen this ratio stand true time and time again. Let it be getting girls (20 approaches at the bar, leads to 4 dates, which results in 1 girlfriend) or jobs (20 job prospects, leads to 4 interviews, which results in 1 offer) or sales calls (20 cold calls leads to 4 follow-ups, leads to 1 closed sale). Just think about it. Who were the guys that had the most success with the ladies in college? Probably your frat bro that didn't give a shit and would talk to any girl that walked in the house.

I'm not telling you to lower your standards and take any girl (job) that falls into your lap. What I am saying is to be comfortable with rejection because it will happen time and time again and will ultimately lead you to where you want to go. Approach that 9.5 at the grocery store. Apply to that job at Goldman Sachs. Cold-call that CEO on the off-chance you can close a sale.

The most successful people in this world have failed a lot. I mean Michael Jordan even failed to make his varsity basketball team until his junior year of high school.

To go along with cliché sports analogies, Wayne Gretzky always says, "You miss 100% of the shots you don't take." Average people don't fail because they don't take risks. *You are not average.*

The more you get rejected the more you learn from that experience. If you want to find that dream job (girl), go for it! And if you get rejected, try again! Because guess what? You will eventually be successful and happy that you took a chance.

HOW TO USE YOUR PHONE LIKE A REAL PERSON

T he average American spends 24 hours a week on their phone in some capacity. This is an entire day gone that you could have spent doing activities you enjoy. *A phone can be the single biggest productivity killer, or when used properly, a tool to help you get through life's daily tasks*. The choice is yours. Most people subconsciously choose the former. The goal of this chapter is to make you a part of the elite group that uses their phones efficiently and in a calculated manner.

Here is a list of apps that you need to download immediately. They will save you a ton money, time, and angst:

- **Venmo:** Securely transfers money regardless of which bank you use. If you don't have this app by now we have bigger problems.
- **Splitwise:** Splits expenses using Venmo. Everyone in a group logs how much they spent on a shared expense and the app does the math for you. Huge for weekend trips when you have one person buying groceries, another buying booze, etc. for a large group.
- **Genius Scan:** Takes pictures and automatically converts them to PDFs. This eliminates the whole "Oh sign this document and fax it back to me" issue. Genius Scan removes the need to ever have a scanner or fax machine.
- **Yelp:** Quickly finds the best restaurants in town. I highly recommend going into your settings and filtering by "Most Reviewed' opposed to "Best

Match" when searching for new spots. If a restaurant is reviewed frequently that means it is popular and a solid choice.

- **Google Maps:** Apple Maps will send you across the country to a Dave & Buster's when you're trying to find your local barber shop. For the love of God please don't use Apple Maps.

Although these apps are essential, I want to warn you against downloading too many apps. Apps can be an unnecessary distraction. I recently deleted all social media from my phone because I found myself subconsciously getting off task. I do not think you need to go to this extreme, but here are a few tips to make sure your phone doesn't take over your life:

- **Limit the amount of times you check your phone in a day**. I know it is hard. Trust me, I literally just threw my phone across the room to concentrate on writing this chapter. I have found the best way to do this is to put your phone in a different room or turn it on airplane mode (See Chapter "Set Yourself Free with Airplane Mode.")
- **Turn off push notifications**. *THIS IS A MUST*. Studies have found the most successful people are those that can concentrate on one task at a time. Having your phone buzz for every Patriots touchdown (I was going to use the Browns, but let's be honest it wouldn't ring that frequently) not only crushes your battery, but leaves you wondering what you were doing before checking your phone. It isn't the ten seconds it takes to check your phone that's terrible, it is getting back into what you were doing that takes the most time.
- **Organize your apps into folders.** Scrolling through 4 screens to find an app is annoying. I have found it's easiest to keep all of my apps in folders in a way that makes sense to find them quickly. For example I have a folder labeled 'Travel' that includes Uber, Google Maps, United Airlines, etc.

Now that we've talked through what apps to download, and tricks to not spending too much time on your phone, here are a few tips on how to get the most out of your phone:

- **Set Reminders:** Most people carry their phone everywhere, so what better tool to remind you to pick up your dry cleaning? I set reminders daily for tasks small and large. For example, I have a reminder set on my phone for the first of every month to write a rent check (landlord doesn't accept Venmo, don't get me started).
- **Take Notes:** This one is very important. How often do you think of a good idea and not write it down? Or how about going to a party and forgetting a

girl's name that you've met 10 times? Nowadays this inexcusable because everyone has a notepad in their pocket. I use my notes application to track everything from life goals, to what to get my girlfriend for Christmas when she drops not so subtle hints, to people's names I should know, to restaurants my barber told me to check out, to my win/loss record in NHL '15 against Jack (as of 10/4/18 I am up 129 to 113. Yes, we've played 242 games since living together). I'm sure you got it by this point, but having notes with you all the time is a life saver.

EAT LUNCH AT 11:45 AM

I'm sure you have picked up on it at this point, but a common theme of this book is efficiency. I constantly think, "Okay, there are twenty-four hours in the day. How can I squeeze as much as I can into those hours?" *One way I have been able to add time back to my day is by completing tasks while others are not.*

People are creatures of habit. I would love to see the statistics on this, but you will find in the working world, most people eat lunch at exactly noon each day. Makes sense--it is right in the middle of an 8 hour work day and it is in poor taste for someone to schedule a meeting during the universally accepted hour for lunch. However, have you ever tried to grab a sandwich during peak lunch hour? It is an absolute zoo and you end up spending more time in line than eating or catching up with co-workers.

I have recently implemented the 11:45 AM lunch and it has changed my life. For someone that is forced to eat out for every lunch (comes with being a consultant), I have observed drastically different size lines at the exact same lunch spots at 11:45am vs. at 12:00pm. Now opposed to spending time in lines, I spend more time eating and recharging for the rest of the work day.

The 11:45 AM lunch is just one example. *I recommend evaluating all your tasks and seeing which ones can be completed quicker by simply switching the time you accomplish those tasks.* Here are a few examples that I have started doing myself:

GOING TO THE GYM AT 5 AM OPPOSED TO AFTER WORK

FYI everyone and their mother does chest day after work on Mondays. Bump chest day back to Wednesday or go in the morning in all hopes of finding a bench.

GROCERY SHOP BEFORE WORK OR IN THE MIDDLE OF THE WEEK

Crazy concept I know, but it is amazing how many people buy groceries Sunday or Monday night. You'll spend just as much time waiting in the checkout line as buying groceries. Grocery shop at 7am on a Wednesday, however, and you might have the whole store to yourself.

FLY ON TUESDAY OR WEDNESDAY

Not only is it cheaper to fly in the middle of the week, but you will avoid the chaos of all the business travelers on Mondays and Thursdays (See Chapter "How to Fly Like a Bo$$"). Of course, given work obligations, not everyone can pull this off. But if you do have a flexible work schedule, flights don't get cheaper or more convenient than in the middle of a week.

WRITE A HANDWRITTEN NOTE ONCE A MONTH

Nowadays no one writes letters. If you want to stand out, be viewed as a leader, and strengthen friendships, start writing notes. Twenty minutes can end up making someone's day (or year) and earning you a lifelong friend.

I recently wrote letters to some of my closest friends telling them how much they meant to me. Most of them responded with how my letter brought them to tears and that they will keep it the rest of their life.

I recommend keeping a list on your phone (See Chapter "How to Use Your Phone Like a Real Person") of people you'd like to write letters to. Spontaneously during my days, I'll think of someone I want to write to and jot it down in my phone. Then when my calendar event pops up monthly for letter-writing, I have a plethora of people I care deeply about to choose from.

Not only will writing a handwritten letter once/month leave the recipient feeling great about themselves, it also will make you feel great to send it. Writing a letter these days may be unusual, but it's a powerful exercise that truly is a win-win for both sides.

IT'S AMAZING WHAT CAN HAPPEN IF YOU "JUST ASK"

OH SO CLOSE TO GOLD STATUS (AS TOLD BY JOEY)

In order to earn Gold Status on United Airlines you need to fly 50,000 miles in a calendar year. Imagine flying 47,000 that year and being just 3,000 measly miles short of achieving status. Most people would say, "Better luck next year" and spend the next 365 days flying in the middle seat next to the toilets. Not me. I wanted the extra legroom and warm breakfast when I flew. So I decided to do what most people wouldn't dare: pick up the phone and call United Airlines...

Long story short, I got 3,000 miles deposited to my account and Gold Status for the next year by simply asking United if they could help me out. *People in a position of power like helping others when they can. The problem is people are often afraid to ask due to fear of rejection.* In my scenario, what's the worst that could have happened? United to say "tough luck, you didn't meet the mileage requirement"? That's not too bad. I would have been in the same position I was before the call.

This is one small example of the benefits of just asking.

CAL NEWPORT (AS TOLD BY JACK)

In the spring of 2008 I stumbled across an author named Cal Newport. He wrote several books on high-performing students and I read and re-read his books religiously. He was (and still is) my favorite author.

Fast-forward to the summer of 2013. I had an internship in Washington, DC. One day I was reading up on Cal Newport (as any normal fan would, not weird in the slightest) and learned he was a computer science professor at Georgetown--just down the road from where I lived.

Well, I had nothing to lose--I scrounged the internet for any contact information I could find and ended up finding his school email address. I wrote him one of those "you probably will never read this but I am a big fan..." emails.

Well, what do you know? Fast forward a couple of weeks and there I was at a coffee shop in Georgetown sitting across the table from my favorite author of all time, starry-eyed, dog-eared books in hand. We chatted for almost an hour and still keep in touch to this day. He even signed my book:

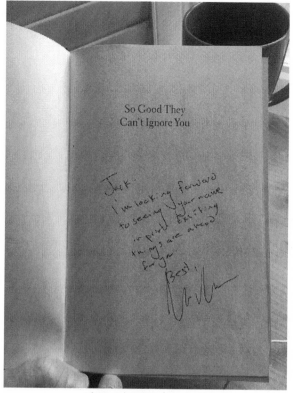

Cal Newport's signature! August 2013

* * *

The point of these stories isn't to brag about our good fortune. The point is this: you would be surprised what you can pull off if you *just ask*. And sure, it will lead to times when you are flat out rejected. But even then, you are right back in the same spot as when you started.

Ask and you shall receive much more often than you'd think.

GIVE YOURSELF TIME IN THE MORNING

I n college, it's easy to set your alarm for 15 minutes before class, get dressed and make it to your first class of the day.

In the real world, you may even be able to do the same for work. The only difference? Work doesn't end after a 50-minute lecture. It goes all day long. There's no nice break between 10am and 11am to "get your life together." In the real world, once you get to work, its *go, go, go* all day.

Therefore, you have to adjust. There are two ways to adjust:

1. **You understand that you won't have a nice mid-morning break and just accept that you won't be able to really plan your day.** You'll run through your work days in a constant "fire drill" state because there are no plans. This is the option that 90% of your peers will choose.

2. **You understand that you won't have a nice mid-morning break and realize the serious value in giving yourself time to "get your life together." Therefore, you wake up earlier.** This is the option we recommend you choose.

I can't stress enough how beneficial it is to wake up 45 minutes before you absolutely have to. And I know the #1 response to this so I'll nip it in the bud right here: "But sleep is healthy. I absolutely need to have my sleep to perform my best!"

You know what you also need to perform your best? A clear head and focused plan every day *before* you step into the office.

My recommendation for balancing sleep with waking up early: find your exact amount of time you need to feel 100%. It might be 8 hours, it might be 7, it might be 6 (if this is you, I am jealous). Prioritize getting that amount of sleep every night. After that, your second priority, ahead of everything else, should be getting up 45 minutes before you absolutely have to. In the next chapter, I'll give you some more tips on possible morning routine activities.

Have trouble with the snooze button in the morning? Put your phone all the way across the room when you charge it at night. You'll be forced to physically get out of bed to turn off your morning alarm and once you're out of bed, you are much more likely to stay that way.

You win the morning, you win the day. 45 minutes of extra time in the morning is the difference between crushing the day and letting the day crush you.

THE UNIVERSAL METHOD TO COMBAT ANY HANGOVER: THE MORNING ROUTINE

S o, now that you've read the previous chapter (if you haven't, flip back a couple pages and read it. It just works better that way), what exactly should you do with your free time in the morning?

As someone famous once said, "You win the morning, you win the day." So let's cut to the chase: the #1 way to win the morning every damn day is with a *morning routine*. Many of the most successful people in the world complete a morning routine...you can too.

Morning Routine (5am to 6:30am)
*7 hours sleep trumps all. If you cannot wake up at 5am and get 7 hours sleep, wake up later & push schedule back.

- ❏ Audible "Let's Go"
- ❏ Make bed
- ❏ Bathroom: Cold water on face, weight
- ❏ 40 push ups
- ❏ Say hi to Casey
- ❏ Thankful book. Ask yourself: "What's really important?"
- ❏ Vitamins, Creatine
- ❏ Shower & brush teeth
- ❏ Daily affirmations in mirror
- ❏ Get dressed
- ❏ Pour coffee (black)
- ❏ 10 min meditation OR outside walk around the block
- ❏ Read
- ❏ Smile, think about family, think about how lucky you are, go crush the day!

Jack's actual morning routine (feel free to steal any parts of it!)

This is my actual morning routine.. I alter it slightly from year to year, but for the most part it stays relatively consistent.

Whether it's the worst of days or the best of days, my day starts the same way. And yours should too.

Every. Single. Day.

A morning routine clears the mind, organizes your life, and gives purpose to your days. Ever wake up in the morning and think "what am I going to do right now, as soon as I get out of bed?" Am I going to make coffee first or brush my teeth? Read the newspaper or answer emails? Take the dog out or organize my calendar? Shower or check my newsfeed? (or do both at the same time, with one arm out of the shower, because you can't decide)?

These decisions reduce our willpower unnecessarily and, for this reason, are decisions you should no longer make.

I'm not going to sit here and tell you what should be in your morning routine and what shouldn't. That's entirely up to you. But If you're going to give a morning routine a try, I have two suggestions:

- **Write It All Down.** If you write down your morning routine, you'll use significantly less willpower to actually complete it each morning. You won't have to think about the order of events in your routine each morning. Think about them once, write them down, and then just follow your own steps!
- **Do It for 21 Days**. Studies show this is how long it takes to form a habit. Don't bail on the morning routine until you have successfully completed it for 3 weeks. Once a habit, it will be significantly easier to tackle in the morning.

BUT WHAT IF I CAN'T COMPLETE MY ROUTINE *EVERY* MORNING?

I often find it hard to complete my entire morning routine. Sometimes it is nearly impossible if I am traveling. It's important to adapt. Find the one or two most critical components of your morning routine and do them no matter the circumstance. It may take only 30 seconds. Do it. The fact that you actively think to do it keeps the 21-day clock running.

After three weeks, you'll get to a Zen-like phase, using next-to-zero willpower, while at the same time setting yourself up for success each and every day.

MY ROUTINE: A COUPLE OF HIGHLIGHTS (AS TOLD BY JACK)

- **Audible "Let's Go":** I don't care if it's 4:30am. I guarantee if you yell this as loud as possible at the ceiling, you will instantly lose all desire to hit the snooze button.
- **Say hi to Casey:** I don't care how bad of a day you've had or how bad of a day you think it's going to be. Think of someone, living or no longer with us, whom you care about deeply. Do so until you can't help but smile. Now the day suddenly doesn't seem that bad anymore, does it?
- **One chapter of a life book:** life's too short to sweat the small stuff.

One of our favorite books, "Don't Sweat The Small Stuff"

DON'T KNOW WHERE TO START?

So you want to give this a try but don't know where to start. Here you go:

Steal my routine. Steal the whole thing. I don't care. It's not copyrighted. I'm not going to sue you. Try it out, then adapt. Hate the whole "yell at the ceiling so loudly your neighbors might just call 9-1-1" step? Take it out. Instead of coffee, do you like to crush a 16-ounce porterhouse steak every morning? Put it in there. *Personalize your routine so you will actually enjoy doing it.* No one else has to do it but you. No one else will see it but you.

Your routine is for your eyes only.

Well, actually, that's what I thought until I wrote this chapter.

DO AT LEAST ONE PHYSICALLY-TAXING TEAM EVENT

... And Pack the Right Food For It

We all have that one friend on Facebook that only posts about his most recent Ragnar, Spartan Race, or Tough Mudder. The cult-like following that comes with these team races single handedly turned me off from participating in one for years. The team-race hardos will always be there, but trust me these events are way more fun than you think and will lead to lifelong memories.

Here are a few reasons why I feel like everyone should participate in at least one physically-taxing team race:

TEAM ACCOMPLISHMENTS BRING YOU CLOSE

There's something about running 202 miles and sleeping in a van with someone that brings you closer than any other activity. For a lot of people, this is the most physically demanding accomplishment of their life. The fact that you were there rooting them on the whole way, will create a bond that can't be duplicated in other settings.

IT LOOKS GOOD ON A RESUME

If you don't have an "Activities & Interests" section of your resume, drop this book and add it right now. This is how an interviewer will get to know you as a person and a lot of times what seals the job. Here is a screenshot from my resume to give you an idea of what I'm talking about:

ACTIVITIES & INTERESTS
- *Type-II Fun:* Tough Mudder & Ragnar alum; biked Pacific Coast Highway (158 miles) with my dad in August 2018
- *Non-Fiction Author: Lessons for Our Younger Brothers* (publish date: Dec 2018)
- *Cleveland Sports:* I live (and die) with the Browns

Joey's Resume

If by the off chance your interviewer has participated in one of these races, it's a done deal and your chances of a job offer increase exponentially. The comradery that comes with these races stretches beyond your team, and it's almost like a fraternity where alumni want to help other alumni out.

IT'S ACTUALLY FUN

When is the last time you've been on monkey bars above a huge pit of mud? Sounds ridiculous, but these races bring you back to your childhood and create a sense of lighthearted fun that you haven't experienced since the playground.

* * *

Finally, if you do decide to participate in one of these events, make sure to pack the right food. In 2016, Jack and I completed a Ragnar (with 10 other friends) where we ran from Madison, Wisconsin to Chicago, Illinois. It was basically 30 hours of running and all we packed was fruit and protein bars (because we didn't want to get full and cramp up). This was a big mistake as it made the run 10 times harder and I ended up losing 13 lbs afterwards. Be smarter than us and don't eat bird food when running across state lines.

EXPECTATION SETTING

*B*eing transparent with people is one of the most underrated ways to gain friends and avoid conflicts. Setting expectations (ahead of time) is something you should do in your professional and personal life to ensure everyone is on the same page.

From a professional standpoint, I always have an expectations conversation with my supervisor every time I start a new project. During this conversation, I clearly state what I want to gain out of the project, my working style, and what motivates me. An example of something I always discuss with my boss is my need to exercise after work. I set the expectation that I will not be available from 5 - 7 pm as I use this time to workout, clear my mind, and reboot for the evening. This way when a 6 pm fire drill comes up and my boss can't reach me via email, he/she is aware where I am and knows I will be back online later in the evening to address the problem.

In your personal life, there are so many times when feelings are hurt because of a lack of communication. A good example is when someone invites you to a group dinner that you don't want to attend. Most people will just ignore the RSVP text in hopes that the host won't get offended by your absence. In reality, the host really just wants to know how much food to cook and would be more pissed if you didn't respond and he ended up making food for you. In this scenario, you should set expectations with the host and tell them you don't plan on attending. This will save an unnecessary disagreement, and free you up to do what you planned on doing instead.

It takes a mature individual to set expectations ahead of time, regardless of the situation. Even if it may be slightly uncomfortable in the moment to set expectations, we promise it will be significantly more uncomfortable if you wait until the last second. Set expectations ahead of time and save yourself from a difficult situation down the road.

SET YOURSELF FREE
WITH AIRPLANE MODE

Texts, emails, calls, voicemails, Instagram, Facebook, Snapchat, ESPN scores, Wikipedia rabbit holes...these days it's all accessible at all times on those tiny computers in your pocket. If you've followed our earlier advice, you've already turned off your push notifications (see "How To Use Your Phone Like a Real Person") but sometimes, that's not enough. You need to set yourself *free*.

So whether you need to make it a weekly habit (Sundays are a great day of the week for airplane mode) or it's just once every so often, we give you permission to *embrace the power of airplane mode*. It will be uncomfortable for a little while, but after an hour or so, your desire to reach for your phone every minute will cease and with this will enter a much more peaceful mental state.

The great thing about airplane mode (vs. turning your phone off entirely) is it still allows you to use basic functions on your phone such as the clock, camera, calculator etc but you can still actually *live in the moment*.

Feeling extra daring? The next time you go on vacation, whether for a day or a week, see if you can turn your phone on airplane mode *for the entire vacation*. We try to do this whenever we can. Trust us--very quickly you'll enter a whole new in-the-moment mental state that is truly refreshing and rewarding.

You don't have to be on an airplane to go on airplane mode...use this knack whenever you need some time "off the grid" or just need to focus on one single task without interruption.

IF YOU BUILD IT THEY WILL COME

In the movie *Field of Dreams*, Kevin Costner famously hears "If you build it, they will come" referring to building a baseball field (for players to come play ball). Little did the *Field of Dreams* movie directors know just how much we would take this phrase to heart...not for building baseball fields, but for building social events.

Here's the thing about being fresh out of college: if you aren't working, you are actively looking for something to do. There really is no in between. You haven't hit the stage of life where you start thinking about bigger things yet (having a family, buying a house, settling down etc.) It really is either work or play for most young and mid 20-somethings.

If there is nothing scheduled, "play" usually consists of heading to the nearest neighborhood bar and seeing where the night takes you. The truth is, no one actually wants this. They'd much prefer to partake in a more organized social event. But 95% of people stop there and hope for someone to organize something. Well we're here to give you permission to be the 5%. *Organize social events and people will come.* How do we know? We did it a time or two...

Ski Party (Denver), Wet Hot American Summer (DC), Indy 500 (Indy), Pond Hockey Classic (Burlington, VT)

"Okay--the pictures have me fired up. I want in. I want to be an organizer. I want to build epic events that people will attend. Where do I start?" Ultimately, it's up to you. There's no rulebook on how to organize events. With that said, here are a few tips we think should help you kick start the process:

FACEBOOK IS ONLY GOOD FOR ONE THING ANYMORE—EVENTS

But it's really good at it. Want to immediately give an upcoming event clout? Make a Facebook event. And do it weeks ahead of time. Not only does this block a date off on the calendar but, when people see that others are "attending," the event builds momentum.

POST ON SAID EVENT MULTIPLE TIMES

I'm sure you've seen this scenario before: someone invites you to a Facebook event 3 weeks ahead of time. It looks fun and you click "attending." Then...radio silence. You assume the event is no longer happening. An hour before the event, the host posts "Can't wait to see you all tonight!" The only problem is you've made other plans. So has everyone else. Everyone assumed the event was no longer happening. Whether you like it or not, guests need intermittent updates between initial event invite and the invite day...they need to know the event is still happening and there will be strong attendance. Example:

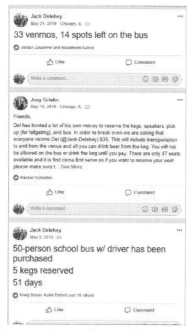

Summer 2016. Jimmy Buffet Concert & Tailgate. 122 Attendees.

Those posts took all of 5 minutes to write and it *guaranteed* everyone at least understood that "Yes, this party is, in fact happening." Now--how do you ensure people think the party is, in fact, going to be worthy of attendance? See below.

IT'S NOT LYING...IT'S JUST PREDICTING THE FUTURE

That screenshot above? I made it all up. No bus was purchased. I hadn't ordered 5 kegs. But guess what? By the time the event rolled around, we had *two* school buses and 7 *kegs*. I know your mother always told you lying was bad...but we're not your mom. When it comes to organizing social events, a little white-lie can go a long way. Why? FOMO. Fear. Of. Missing. Out. People see an epic party opportunity (and one that is continuously being updated) and they don't want to miss out. So they commit. So do a lot of people. And before you know it, you do have enough to fill a school bus (just like you knew you would). If you don't like to call it lying, you can tell yourself it is just "predicting the future." You just so happen to claim it is now. You have permission to lie in order to hype up your event...just make sure you follow through.

COLLECT PAYMENT AHEAD OF TIME...AND SET ARBITRARY DEADLINES TO DO SO

No one will pay without arbitrary deadlines. And you need payment to host large group events. Set arbitrary deadlines and stick to them. Post often about the upcoming deadline. You'd be surprised at how well this works (collect via Venmo, of course).

THE MORNING-OF POST

This right here puts you in an elite echelon. You do this and you are the Tom Brady of party hosting. Ex: You've done a fantastic job of hyping a party for the past couple of weeks. You've followed these instructions, posted every few days with updates, instilled an arbitrary deadline to collect payments, and have a solid attending list. It's the morning of your party and you need one more hype post, one more post to possibly shift those "Maybes" over to the "Attending" category. 10 or 20 more last-second attendees are absolutely attainable. But how do you do it?

Post a photo of an early-attending person at your party, ideally female. Females enjoy the presence of other females. We've all been to those parties with 20 males and 1 female. And the truth is females do not feel comfortable at parties like these. Parties are about establishing clout and comfortability. There is no better way to establish clout and comfortability than show that a fun person deems your party worthy of attendance. Example:

Jack Delehey
June 29

Keg is tapped, food is on the grill, come one come all.

Shout out to Dev!

If hosting parties isn't your thing, we completely understand. But if done well, hosting people can be a ton of fun, can drastically increase your social network, and is *way, way* cheaper than going out to bars. The next time you decide to host, give these tips a try. You won't be disappointed.

LEAD IN EVERY ASPECT OF YOUR LIFE

E veryone wants to become a CEO. Society portrays the path to leadership as taking on more responsibility at work, finding younger colleagues to coach, and making your way up the corporate ladder. *What people don't understand is the C-Suite at their company didn't get their leadership skills by rising through the ranks at work. In a way, it's really the opposite. These leaders got to where they are because they developed leadership skills early on and used them to succeed at the office.* Let me explain.

There are a few natural born leaders. These are unicorns. Most of us have to develop these skills over years and years of practice. Unless you are the beneficiary of some serious nepotism and get a leadership role out of college, most of us won't get the opportunity to lead a large team at work until a minimum of 5 years post-graduation.

"I don't want to wait that long, how can I develop leadership traits earlier on?" Good question.

The trick to developing leadership skills at a young age is by actively leading in your personal life. You can establish yourself as a leader amongst your friend group by simply organizing a party or dinner for a large group of people (See Chapter "If You Build It, They Will Come"). Most of your friends will shy away from this task because it requires coordination, foresight, and dealing with differing personalities/preferences. *This is what leaders do! You should hop at these opportunities because it allows you to practice being a leader in a low-consequence environment.* If you bring the group to a burger joint and someone is vegan, it's not the end of the world.

Your friends are going to look at you in a more favorable light for volunteering, and you will get the added benefit of perfecting your leadership skills.
I advise you to find any way possible to lead in different aspects of your life because these skills will translate to the working world. You will be more confident taking on leadership roles at work as you have practiced doing so time and time again with your peers.

So the next time your friends want to plan a weekend trip to the beach, take the reins. Who knows, maybe you'll develop a lifelong skill that lands you a seat at the executive table someday.

THE ONLY 4 BOOKS YOU NEED TO READ

1. *4-Hour Workweek* by Tim Ferris
2. *Money Master the Game: 7 Simple Steps to Financial Freedom* by Tony Robbins
3. *Don't Sweat the Small Stuff and It's All Small Stuff: Simple Ways to Keep The Little Things From Taking Over Your Life* by Richard Carlson
4. *How to Win Friends and Influence People* by Dale Carnegie

These books changed our lives. It would be a mistake not to read them.

HOW TO MOVE UP THE CORPORATE LADDER

You want to find success in corporate America? I'm going to let you in on three simple steps to climb the corporate ladder and get promoted faster than your peers:

GET LUCKY

This is out of your control. It sucks. A lot of moving up is being at the right place at the right time. The people I know that have gotten promoted on accelerated timeframes have gotten lucky in one way or another; let it be their supervisor going on paternity leave forcing them into a stretch role or having a mentor that takes them under their wing. As much as you can't control luck, *you can put yourself in positions to get lucky.* When you recognize you are getting lucky, make sure you capitalize, as these situations don't come by every day.

BE SLIGHTLY ABOVE AVERAGE AT YOUR JOB

There is a misconception that corporate leaders get to where they are because they were the highest performers at the lower ranks. This is not necessarily true (see the "Lead in Every Aspect of Your Life" chapter). You do not have to be the #1 shining star to be successful, but you do have to be above average. (Note: there is nothing wrong with working extremely hard and performing exceptionally at your job. In fact, there are many advantages of doing so. But the purpose of this chapter is to describe how to get promoted, not how to be the next Steve Jobs. If you have greater aspirations than promotion, we applaud you.) Do enough to be viewed as a hard worker that produces good work, but what's really important for your success is the next step.

HAVE HIGHER UP PEOPLE LIKE YOU

This is the single greatest contributor to your success in corporate America. If people like you; you will get promoted. It's that simple. As much as you don't want to go to that leadership luncheon; not only attend, but do something to make a connection with your superiors. There is a lot of ways to get your bosses to like you (read *How To Win Friends and Influence People* for tips), but what I have found to be the most effective is showing you work your ass off and getting to know them on a personal level. This often involves dedicating your free time after work. Find what makes your bosses tick on a personal level and use this to connect to them. Yes, this takes effort, but it will make you stand out and pay dividends for the remainder of your career.

TURN OFF OUTLOOK NOTIFICATIONS

I f we had a Book of Corporate World Commandments (sequel?), commandment #1, #2, and #3 would all be "Thou shalt not be held captive by Outlook email notifications."

Cal Newport, one of the all-time productivity GOATs out there, classifies distraction-free work as "Deep Work." Not only is Deep Work vital in this world of constant connectedness, but it is becoming increasingly rare by the day. And one of the biggest reasons Deep Work is becoming more and more difficult is people are inundated with emails.

We truly hope you do not see this hundreds of times per day...

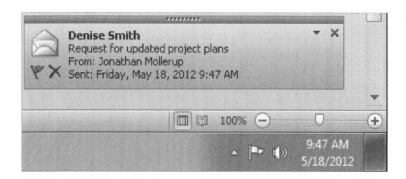

But if you do, it's time to turn off your Outlook notifications immediately.

COMMON CONCERN: "BUT I CAN'T! WHAT IF I MISS AN IMPORTANT EMAIL AND MY BOSS IS UPSET?"

- **Expectation Set with your Boss**: See Chapter "Expectation Setting" for more insight here. Ask your boss proactively for a meeting. In the meeting describe the reasons you are proposing turning off your Outlook notifications (i.e. you want to be more efficient, i.e. you want to *help the company make more money*). 99% of bosses will be incredibly impressed with both your proactive nature and your thoughtfulness. If your boss falls into the 1% that is so stuck in their ways, they blindly follow corporate rules and need you to always be "online," then I recommend searching for job opportunities that value proactive efficiency.

- **Set a rule to only notify you when specific individuals email you.** A possible response from your boss might be, "Okay, I am fine with you turning off Outlook notifications...but you need to respond to *my* inquiries immediately." This is reasonable. After all, he is your boss. A quick google search will yield step-by-step instructions on how to set inbox rules so you only receive notifications when certain individuals send you emails. This is a life-saver and will keep your boss happy and you efficient.

Don't be held captive by Outlook. Set restrictions proactively and you'll turn a nuisance into a valuable tool you can use *on your terms.*

DON'T GET SCREWED BY FREE 30-DAY TRIALS

These days it seems every company offers free 30-day trials. And without realizing it, that free 30-day trial turns into an expensive recurring payment. Don't let the companies win! Mark the end date to the free trial on your calendar (see "Calendar is Key" chapter if you don't yet have a calendar) the moment you sign up. To be extra safe, give yourself a few days buffer and mark the free trial end date for day 27 or 28. That way you won't have to randomly remember to cancel your free trial...your calendar will remember for you.

ALREADY HAVE TOO MANY SUBSCRIPTIONS TO COUNT?

Cancel Your Credit Cards and You'll Find Out Which Ones You Actually Want to Keep

After 30 days you'll get the "your credit card cannot be processed" emails. It's an easy way to really, truthfully decide if the subscription is worth it.

Don't want to go through the hassle of canceling credit cards? Try the Hiatus App!

PARTY TROLLEYS ARE A MARKET INEFFICIENCY...TAKE ADVANTAGE

Once upon a time you were in college. In fact, you still may be in college. If you are, enjoy it while it lasts. You are surrounded by peers your age, half of whom you could potentially have a romantic relationship with. Additionally, you already have *at least one thing in common: you attend the same school.* Why is this important? Because everyone wants to feel comfortable in a romantic relationship. An immediate way to feel comfortable is to have a characteristic in common.

Real world update: in any given bar, most people you meet did not, in fact, go to your college! This seems obvious, of course. But the bigger point here is the time it takes up front to court a complete stranger you might be interested in is much, much longer in the real world. After all, they have no idea who you are, where you come from, what your background is etc. If you see a cute girl across the bar, mathematically speaking, the odds are low you can randomly approach that female, introduce yourself, establish a connection, gain trust, and end up dating her down the line. Not impossible (and certainly worth the shot) but much, much less likely than the exact same situation when you were a 21-year old college junior at your local college bar.

However, there's a real-world cheat-code: Party Trolleys.

WHAT'S A PARTY TROLLEY?

In short, Party Trolleys are large moving vehicles (either literally a trolley car or, more often, a bus) that are wide-open with seats around the edge.

Most major cities have several party trolley companies (shout out to Tom at Premier Trolley & Limo in Chicago--legends). These trolleys typically hold anywhere from 25-40 people and have the same types of liquor licences as limos (aka you can drink on them legally while the trolley is moving).

WHY IS A PARTY TROLLEY SO GREAT?

Party trolleys have the following ideal components for meeting those of the opposite gender (or same gender--it's 2018 after all and we certainly support all types of relationships!) In our time of party-trolleying, we saw no less than 5 couples begin their relationships with a trolley. Seriously. Characteristics:

1. **It's Unique**: People don't just do party trolleys all the time. Everyone loves something unique and cool.
2. **It's a Hell of a Time**: To be blunt, party trolleys are ridiculously fun.

3. **Alcohol is Allowed on the Trolley**: Self-explanatory.
4. **It's Chaotic**: People are constantly moving around on party trolleys. This leads to the possibility of conversations with lots of people. (Opposite of this: A "big" group dinner at a long table where you can only speak to the person on your right and left).
5. And, the last component that is absolutely the most crucial component: **Party trolleys require the exact perfect amount of people on them. They require more people than a core friend group, but not so many people that there are truly random "strangers" at the event.**
    a. In the real world, many eventual relationships come from friends of friends (see above: comfortability). And party trolleys are *full* of them. 25-40 people is too many for one single core group of friends. So friends have to reach out to secondary friends and friends-of-friends. If there were 150 people on a trolley, people wouldn't feel comfortable. But 25-40 and everyone is comfortable. Everyone on the trolley is either a very good friend or a very good friends' friend. Therefore, *everyone on the trolley is inherently socially comfortable with each other, regardless of if they consciously realize this fact.*

We have probably hosted no less than a dozen trolley events in our life. I truly cannot think of a single one in which *multiple people* didn't end up "finding someone great." Time and time again, party trolleys never failed. And it makes perfect sense! Combine a little bit of alcohol with a lot of awesome friends, some of whom are secondary friends, and you have the perfect combination for romance.

Now, it would be a travesty to leave this chapter without mentioning the fact that party trolleys are incredible regardless of this romantic factor. So if you're locked up with a girlfriend or not even looking for one, it doesn't matter. Some of our fondest memories of our early 20's are on party trolleys.

Party trolleys are a market inefficiency. They are underutilized and undervalued. Host one and we guarantee it won't be your last.

Chicago Party Trolley. July 2016.

HOW TO NOT GET FAT
IN 3 SIMPLE STEPS

Everyone claims they are going to get in shape after they graduate. "Well there's no way I will be drinking more beers than I am right now, so after I walk for graduation I will start hitting the gym." I've heard it time and time again. Well here's a newsflash: In the real world you have significantly less time than you do in college and *most of my friends actually got fatter post fraternity life.*

Sounds impossible right? Not if you think about it. During college you are constantly walking to class, playing intramural sports, and sneaking in the occasional chest day. In the real world you are sitting at a desk for 8 hours and only getting up to get a cup of coffee or walk to your car to drive to lunch. By the time you get home, cook dinner, and unwind, there is very little time to get to the gym. In college you have a meal plan where you occasionally sneak in a piece of fruit or a vegetable (I mean you get a million sides, you can only get so many cookies). In the real world you have this new task of cooking, which leads to many nights of pasta and take out burgers.

I'm not going to tell you to stop eating pizza and drinking beer. Both of us agree if you have a six pack in college (or a year or two post college) you're doing it wrong. But I do want to leave you with three simple steps to ensure you don't get fat in your first couple years on your own.

DRINK A TON OF WATER

Not only is water free and the best way to kick a hangover, it is also one of the most effective ways to keep the pounds off. You know how to use Google so I'm not going to go over the health benefits of water. I will, however, let you in on a couple lesser known secrets of pounding H₂0.

First off, *drinking water throughout the day does an amazing job of keeping you full,* which in turn prevents you from diving face first into the corporate snack drawer. I had no idea that you could get full off of water, but if you drink the recommended 3.5 liters a day you will be significantly less hungry. I have found when I drink water, I'm not unbearably hungry come lunch so I don't overeat unhealthy food.

Secondly, crushing water makes you leave your desk to pee. This might sound ridiculous, but there are studies that show *getting up from your desk for as little as 2 minutes can jumpstart your metabolism* and keep you burning calories throughout the day. When you are head down cranking out an analysis the minutes can turn into hours and next thing you know you've been seated in the same position for half the work day. This will not only crush your posture, but will also make you feel sluggish and prevent you from getting exercise at work. Drinking water forces you to go to the bathroom which allows you to get up and walk around when movement in an office is tough to find.

So now go onto Amazon, purchase a Nalgene or HydroFlask and keep it with you all the time. Trust me, you'll start to feel and look better.

EAT UNTIL YOU'RE 80% FULL

I know what you're thinking, "So first you tell me to drink so much water that I trick my body into thinking I'm full and now you're telling me to starve myself? That's not going to fly." Trust me, I think one of the most harmful things for the body are crash diets where you do not get enough nutrients. I do, however, think portion sizes in America are wayyyy too large (if you go to any other country portion sizes are half as big) and people overeat because they eat until they are full opposed to when they are no longer hungry. I will get to this in a minute.

Quick reminder, this chapter is called how not to get fat, opposed to how to get ripped. This language is intentional. If this chapter was about getting ripped I would talk about switching your diet to mostly vegetables, intermittent fasting to put your body into ketosis, and having a proper balance of healthy fats, protein, and macros in your meals. I don't think this is realistic or necessary for your stage in life. I want you to be able to enjoy yourself and eat that burrito at 3 AM. If you follow the advice in this chapter, you can keep the diet you have now, and avoid the "real world 15." Trust me, it's as real as the "freshman 15."

So back to eating until you're 80% full. It is scientifically proven that it takes 15 minutes to feel full after eating. That means if you eat until you are full, you are really eating until you're about to explode. I suggest eating slower and only eating until you are no longer hungry. This way by the time your food digests you will be the perfect amount of full. I found when I started implementing this strategy, I didn't crash after eating lunch. I had more energy for the rest of the day. I follow these rules to this day. Not do I eat the proper amount, but I also am not tired after work so I can enjoy my time at home.

LEARN TO LOVE TO RUN

I know this is by far the hardest of the three. Trust me, running sucks when you first start off. As someone that avoided running for the first 21 years of my life, the last thing I thought I'd be recommending is telling others to run. But after you get past that initial period of getting in running shape, there is nothing more therapeutic or efficient as far as getting the best workout in the shortest period of time.

Please find me someone that runs 6 miles a day and is fat. It doesn't happen. Running is the most efficient way to burn calories and you can get an amazing workout in just 45 minutes. It doesn't take driving to the gym, fancy equipment or anything other than a pair of shoes and some shorts. That is why it is the workout of choice for road warriors that have to travel for work. I guarantee you if you find yourself running consistently you will immediately lose weight and keep it off. When I started running regularly I lost 15 pound and I have kept that weight off ever since.

As great as running is for your physical health, I think it is even better for your mental health. Being able to clear your mind of all life's stresses and concentrate on nothing else is one of the greatest feelings in the world. I have had some of my most clear thoughts running. It's also the best way to re energize yourself after a long work day. I cannot tell you how many times I've worked late into the night trying anything under the moon to keep myself awake. What I have found to be more effective than caffeine or a "twenty minute cat nap" (has anyone ever done this successfully?) is taking a half hour jog around the block. You will come back feeling accomplished, wide awake, and ready to take on any crazy formula Excel has thrown your way.

HOSTING ON AIRBNB IS THE GOAT

Three words: passive income baby. Two more words: free cleaning. Everyone is hesitant to list their place on Airbnb in fear that someone is going to rob them blind or break their most valued possession. First off, Airbnb has crazy insurance policies so you are always protected (up to one million dollars, seriously). Secondly, as someone who has listed their apartment on Airbnb for years, the pros heavily outweigh the cons.

Here are some of the unarguable benefits to Airbnb-ing out your place when not at home:

FREE WEEKEND TRIPS

We used to only host on Airbnb weekends we were not in town. In return, we would be earning money from our apartment while sleeping for free on our friends' couches. The money we collected from Airbnb would more than pay for our trips to visit our friends.

FREE CLEANING

As a host you have the ability to charge whatever you'd like for cleaning. This was a HUGE benefit as we would pay for a professional cleaner to come through any time after hosting folks on Airbnb. There is nothing better than coming back to a spotless apartment.

LITTLE WORK REQUIRED

We had hosting on Airbnb down to a science. We made YouTube videos to answer FAQs and sent the links to our guests (I.E. teaching them how to connect to the Bluetooth). We also had a lockbox where they would pick up the key whenever they got in town (This is absolutely mandatory. You never want to have to hand off the keys and pick them up in person). There were times when we would receive a couple hundred dollars in our bank accounts without ever interacting with a guest. If you are actually considering taking the steps to host on Airbnb, email us and we'll send you several hosting templates we've created to make it as easy as possible for you.

PEOPLE LEAVE SHIT

Yes, guests would occasionally eat out of our fridge or take some of the booze we left around, but more times than not we would come out on top from all the food / beers they'd leave behind. No one is going to fly back home with 9 left over beers in their suitcase.

In short, hosting on Airbnb required very little work, provided us with a spotless apartment, and gave us a little extra spending cash. There is little reason not to do give it a try.

IF YOU FIND A BLOW UP MATTRESS THAT DOESN'T DEFLATE, HOLD ONTO IT LIKE YOUR LIFE DEPENDS ON IT

Household hacks. Something you've never had to think about until now. Living on your own means buying all of the expensive household items that mom always had laying around the house. This includes a vacuum, colander, measuring cups, Swiffer, I mean everything. This might sound daunting and expensive, but it doesn't have to be. A quick Google search will point you in the right direction of items you need to buy and I feel comfortable saying you can buy the cheapest version of 99% of things. However, there are a few household essentials that are worth splurging on now to save angst later. This list includes the following:

BLENDER

I recommend a Ninja or NutriBullet (Ninjas are slightly less expensive). We use our blender literally every day for making smoothies and grounding up healthy ingredients that taste terrible on their own. Oh you don't like the taste/texture of Kale? Ground it up and mix it with peanut butter. Bam, health to the veins. Cheap blenders are tough to clean and leave you with half ground up concoctions that are unbearable to drink. I recommend small/personal blenders because they are muuuuch easier to clean.

NON-STICK PANS

For the love of God buy nice pans. You will use them every day and nothing is more deflating than having to scrape a pan full of eggs for fifteen minutes. Over time non-stick pans start to get sticky. As soon as this happens, throw them out and buy new ones. Pans are relatively cheap and it is so worth it. We buy new frying pans about once a year.

VACUUM

You will not clean if you have to continuously vacuum the same spot because your vacuum sucks at sucking.

AIR MATTRESS

When you are right out of college and living in a new city, all of your friends are going to want to visit. Unless you want them all to pile in bed with you, you're going to have to buy an air mattress. Splurge and buy an expensive one. Also buy a queen size so two normal people (or five tipsy friends desperate for anything other than the floor) can fit on it. Your friends will not come back if it keeps deflating in the middle of the night and they don't get any sleep after being at the bars until 3 AM.

IRON / STEAMER

I don't care which one you get, but you need one or the other. Looking sharp for work is imperative and your colleagues and boss will notice. Buy a nice iron or steamer to make sure you stand out amongst your peers. If you travel often, there are great $30 travel steamers on Amazon. I've had the same one for five years--it is a lifesaver.

IF YOU DON'T HAVE VENMO, YOU ARE NOT ALLOWED TO READ ANOTHER WORD OF THIS BOOK. CLOSE THE BOOK. GO DOWNLOAD VENMO. NOW.

PARENTS ARE THE BEST

Y ou don't know what you have until it's gone. I didn't realize how much I relied on my parents until I was out on my own. As much as college makes you feel independent, your parents are always there to act as a safety net whenever shit hits the fan. Once you graduate and move out, you're truly on your own and you'll come to appreciate how much your parents do for you.

As hard as it is to admit, there's going to be a time when our parents are no longer around. Don't be one of those people that look back and wish they had a better relationship with their parents. Or one of those people that didn't spend enough quality time because they were worried about something that in the larger scheme of life isn't that important (aka work).

Here are some ways to ensure your parents always stay in your life and you make the most out of no longer living under the same roof:

- Routinely fill them in on your life, they live for this (I recommend having a set day you call them each week).
- Just because you're out of the house doesn't mean you can't ask for advice when times are tough. They know you the best and can solve some of your biggest challenges for you.
- Actively invite them to visit you; they want to visit, but don't want to burden you. Make an effort.
- When you are home for the holidays, appreciate how good the food is. Nothing is as good as home cooking. Period.
- Tell your parents how much you appreciate them. Whether you tell them in-person, on Facetime, over the phone or with a handwritten note (See Chapter "Write a Handwritten Note Once A Month") is up to you. But opening up and telling your parents how much they truly mean to you, after

they gave unconditionally to you for 20+ years without asking for anything in return, will absolutely make their day.

TELL YOUR STORY

D o you know why the ACTs and SATs exist? They exist so college admissions representatives have something universal to compare students.

There are no real world ACTs and SATs.

Sure, there are other accolades out there in the real world used to distinguish levels of accomplishment or education ("I am a Chartered Financial Analyst!" "I am a Doctor!") but these levels of accomplishment are spread out across many industries and none are mandatory.

Why do I bring this up? Because when you enter the real world, *there is no longer a universal method for others to assess value.* In a job interview there is no longer a common denominator amongst candidates like there was when applying to college. In college admissions, if two candidates were deemed "equal" and one had a 30 ACT score, the other a 34 ACT score, 10/10 times admissions is taking the second student. But because there is no real world ACT score, it is *extremely important than you learn how to tell your story.* Learning how to tell your story is equally, if not more important, than what you've actually accomplished!

What do I mean? Let's take a look at an example.

JOHN AND JIM

John and Jim are identical twins. Not only that, they pretty much do everything together. Both are 23, both graduated from the same college one year ago and have had an entry level job at the same management consulting firm for the past year. While both have enjoyed some aspects of the role, they've often felt underappreciated and overworked. Both are actively searching for new jobs and have found a great opportunity to which they both apply. The only difference? John has not read this book. Jim has.

John's Resume	Jim's Resume
Work Experience *XYZ Consulting: Analyst – Provide insight & suggestions to clients on more efficient methods of work.	*Work Experience* *XYZ Consulting: Analyst - Worked collaboratively on a team of 25 to provide insight & suggestions to clients on more efficient methods of work. Led initiative that resulted in $2.5M in recurring savings for client.
Education *ABC University, Honors Student	*Education* *ABC University, Honor roll 7 of 8 semesters
Interests *Food, Travel	*Interests* *Food: Nancy's Deep Dish = best in Chicago *Travel: Spent 4 months living in Cape Town

John and Jim completed the exact same work at their management consulting firm. The difference? Jim simply did a better job of demonstrating his value and telling his story! And it only took him 10 extra minutes to craft his descriptors on his resume. As you can imagine, Jim gets the interview. John does not. Not only that, once in the interview, Jim provides a thoughtful story about his life path & why he is interviewing with the specific firm. His story, as told through his resume and interview, ultimately land him the job.

PROACTIVELY SHOW YOUR VALUE

Notice that I've never said Jim is any more capable of actually completing the work at this new job. And that's exactly the point--in the real world you need to proactively show your value. Unlike an SAT/ACT score, value won't necessarily show for itself. In the example above, Jim went the extra mile to *show* his value. John did not and the results speak for themselves.

UNIQUE > DIFFICULT

As you begin thinking about your story and how you want to show your value, keep one important note in mind: *just because something is more difficult does not mean it is more valuable in the eyes of a potential employer. What really stands out is when something is unique, regardless of the difficulty to complete.*

So if you are a senior in college and wondering if you should grind out 7 classes/semester in order to double major, I recommend you think again. Is there something else you could add into your life that may take up significantly less time but is more *unique*? Lots of people double major. It is not unique and also takes up a significant amount of time. Could you perhaps keep your single major and instead start a club on campus?

TWO EXAMPLE STUDENT BACKGROUNDS

- **Student A:** I am a 4th year student double-majoring in Economics and Philosophy.
- **Student B:** I am a 4th year student majoring in Economics. I am also the Founder and President of the Philosophy club on campus, a 12-person organization that meets weekly to discuss relevant readings, life goals, and the meaning of life.

The second example is likely more impressive to an employer *and* takes significantly less time to complete. Additionally, the second bullet is *unique*. Lots of people double-major. Very few people start a Philosophy club. *Just because something is harder to complete does not mean it is more valuable.*

* * *

So as you plan out your next steps in life, whether it be in school or the real world, keep this in mind. Just as important as *what* you do is *how you tell your story.*

HOW TO DO NEW YEARS RIGHT (AND OTHER PARTY HACKS)

L et us paint you a scene: it's December 15th. You get a text from a friend: "Hey, any New Years plans? I found a bar in the city. It's $175, four drinks included. A little pricey but I haven't found anything cheaper..."

Now, if you hadn't read this chapter, you'd probably grit your teeth, respond with a "Yeah, sounds like that's what we should do" and toss two-hundred bones at the event, knowing all too well that you'll likely have minimal amounts of fun due to the over-crowded bar and over-hyped evening in general.

Well, as of now, you officially have permission from us to *actually think about how best to have the most fun at social events*. Notice that in almost every situation there is a common theme: *the pre-party is almost always significantly more fun than the actual party.*

NEW YEARS EVE

The most over-hyped, over-priced evening of the entire year. Instead of tossing $200 to a bar, here's a thought: throw a huge house party, invite all of your friends, and charge 1/10th the amount per person. You'll be surrounded by friends, free drinks and might just actually have fun.

T-BOX (CHICAGO)/SANTA CON (NYC)

Don't go to the event. Stay at the pre-game. Would you rather be surrounded by strangers drinking $12 beers or surrounded by your best friends drinking $1 beers?

CONCERTS

Just because the gates open at 2pm doesn't mean you have to go right in. Ever experience a parking lot party?

* * *

In short, challenge the status quo and think strategically about what the most fun option is. We have a saying, "If you're having fun, why deviate"? In the concert example, if you're having the time of your life in the parking lot, why go to the show? Because you bought a ticket? Your ticket is a sunk cost. Life is too short to not do everything in your power to maximize your happiness. Sometimes that means skipping the main event to finish an epic game of flip cup at the pre-game.

PAY FOR A DEEP CLEAN AT LEAST ONCE EVERY SIX MONTHS

L et's be honest, you can't clean like mom. If you've never dusted or cleaned your toilets since you moved, it's about time to spend $60 on a cleaner. You will feel much better after.

GET TO KNOW THE "SMALL" PEOPLE

Who are the most important people in your daily life? I bet you immediately started thinking about your family and closest group of friends. Yes, these people are unarguably your support system and define who you are as a person. However, the question wasn't who are the most important people in your life, but who are the most important in your *daily* life. I believe these are two different things.

When you graduate from college, move out of the house to live on your own, and start working a corporate job, there is this weird shift that happens to your social network. Up to this point in your life, your day to day has been surrounded by people that love and know you best. Through high school you would see your family every single day. In college, you develop a close group of friends that you see regularly and become a substitute family. Even if you didn't live with these friends there is a good chance they weren't more than a ten minute walk away.

One of the areas I struggled with the most after moving out on my own was the *most important people in my life were no longer in my daily life.* I couldn't just walk to the kitchen to talk to my parents or to the fraternity house to discuss my problems with my friends. Almost over night my network of family and friends went from under the same roof to a plane flight away. This terrified me.

Post graduation life is filled with routines. "Real world" tasks such as going to the grocery store, doing dry cleaning, and getting light bulbs at Home Depot, become regular occurrences. This might sound depressing to a college student whose only plan for the week is attending a paint party on Friday night, but as we discuss throughout this book, routines are healthy and should be embraced. These adult chores result in you running into the same people week in and week out. I'm talking about the dry cleaner that sews your buttons (because your mom used to always do this) or the check-out guy at the grocery store. I would say 99% of people float through their weekly tasks without learning the names or even acknowledging these "small" people. *I challenge you to be in the 1% and not only learn the names of the "small" people in your everyday life, but form genuine relationships with them.* Let me tell you why.

LEARNING THE NAMES OF "SMALL" PEOPLE HAS IT'S FREE PERKS

Imagine having a job that was so routine that you could almost do it subconsciously. Then imagine encountering hundreds if not thousands of people each day doing this job and no one calls you by name (even though you clearly have a name tag on). Pretty miserable, right?

Let's say that this job is a grocery store clerk. Now imagine that someone with a bright smile calls you by name, asks about your son's baseball game, and brings you a piece of cake while you are ringing up their groceries (this is a real scenario). Won't you be more inclined to help this person when they can't find paprika flakes?

Note: Studies show that people love hearing their own name. In fact, it makes their day. I highly recommend keeping a list on your phone of the names of people you interact with on a daily basis. That way, the next time you walk into the gym, you can confidently look the person at the check-in desk in the eye, thank them, and call them by name. I guarantee this thoughtful gesture will brighten up their day.

Back to the story--let me tell you, the perks go beyond paprika flakes. Here are a few examples of free stuff I have gotten by forming relationships with the "small" people:

- **Hotel Room Upgrades:** I got upgraded to an executive suite every week during a project in LA because I would ask the hotel receptionist about his Crossfit training

- **Garage Pass/Apartment Fob:** When moving out of our apartment complex in Denver the receptionist allowed us to keep our garage pass/apartment fob which gave us access to free downtown parking/amazing pool

- **Free Beers/Burgers for Life:** After driving to Denver from Chicago, we were craving burgers so we found the most popular spot in town. The manager loved our spontaneous move across the country and how complimentary we were of the burgers. He not only comped our meal and wrote down a list of his favorite restaurants in Denver, but we have not paid for a single meal/beer since (we have been there 20+ times).

- **All You Can Drink Bud Light Parties:** We went to the same bar every Thursday night our first year in Chicago. They did random raffles where the winner could host a three hour all you can drink Bud Light party for as many friends as you want. Because the bartenders liked us, we'd be "randomly" selected pretty much any time we entered. We had four all you can drink parties and invited 40+ friends each time.

- **Storage:** We had a three month gap between our Chicago lease ending and our Denver lease starting. Opposed to paying hundreds of dollars for a storage unit in Chicago, the handyman we befriended (shout out to Daniel, a true gentleman) at our old apartment turned his head the other way when we stored our mattresses in the basement of the complex for three months.

- **Free Gym in NYC:** My gym membership doesn't work in NYC. Extremely frustrating. But Scott at the Sheraton in Time Square saved me. Not only that, he gave me his personal cell phone to text him whenever I am in town so he can make sure he opens the doors for me!

"SMALL" PEOPLE HELP FILL THE VOID OF MISSING "LARGE" PEOPLE

While your original motive might stem from a combination of your desire to learn people's names *and* your love of free stuff (it's okay, who doesn't love free stuff?), at some point, your relationship with these people will change for the better.

In my experience, I started becoming true, genuine, friends with these "small" people...

I began looking forward to going to the grocery store to strike up a conversation with the employees and excited to drop my dress shirts off at the dry cleaner. My weekly chores became fun and the relationships that started off as transactional became meaningful.

At the beginning of this chapter, I mentioned one of the hardest parts about moving away from home is not having a daily support blanket of family and friends. Not to say the grocery store clerk replaced the comfort of seeing my mother every day, but in a way *encountering friendly familiar faces regularly made it easier to be so far away.* These "small" people helped fill a void for me. So the next time your handy man comes over to fix a pipe, ask him how his kids are doing. You might get a free repair, or even better, a lifelong friend.

WEAR CLOTHING THAT REPRESENTS YOU IN PUBLIC

When you get on an airplane, don't be afraid to rock your college sweater! When you go to a bar, wear that ball-cap of your favorite team. When you're on the golf course, whip out that polo with your high school logo on the front. On the off-chance someone in the vicinity shares a similar interest or recognizes your school colors, they *will* go out of their way to say hi. Worst case the person is cool and you share a beer and go your separate ways.

Best case, it's someone who is cute and you're romantically attracted to and you've just been given the biggest head-start imaginable...

SOMETIMES WHEN YOU'RE AN ADULT YOU PAY FOR SHIT YOU DON'T WANT TO

Just some of the many examples:

- Taxes
- Rent
- Health Insurance
- Renters Insurance
- Business clothes/suits
- Gas for your car (when you start saying "$3.75 a gallon!? That's ridiculous!" you'll understand)
- A fix-it man to come and fix something not covered by your landlord. (Drain-O when your shower drain is clogged is NOT cheap)
- Movers (if you are in a big city like New York)
- Finder's fees for apartments (select cities)

Etc. etc. etc. You've now officially been warned. It sucks. Get used it. It comes with adulthood.

NEVER TURN DOWN A ROAD TRIP

Believe it or not, one day you'll be 50 years old, settled down in the suburbs with a spouse and two kids, and living a pretty routine life. And guess what? You'll absolutely love it. But guess what else you'll also love? Being able to look back on your earlier life and say, with absolute conviction, that you really *lived* life back in the day.

Lucky for you "back in the day" is *now*. How awesome is that? It's not a 25 year old memory...it's today. You really have two options with your early 20's:

1. **Make the most of it.** You'll never be as attractive, financially/socially able, and childless as you are right now.
2. **Not take advantage.** You'd hate to look back on some of the most amazing years of your life knowing you played it safe or grew up too fast (when you get older you'll have a friend that always makes excuses like "I can't go on that trip, I need to save for a house.")

"But I don't really know how or where to find cool stuff, Jack and Joey." - There is a really, really easy way to find cool stuff to do--just start saying "yes" to things. It's amazing what can come out of it.

THE 3 WEEKS RULE (AS TOLD BY JACK)

It was June of 2017 and I was swamped with work. I was exhausted, pulling 14 hour days with no end in sight. And then Joey said, "Hey Del, let's go to Telluride Bluegrass festival this weekend." Ohhhhh no no no. No way. I had a date with my couch and some much needed sleep on the horizon.

But then Joey quickly reminded me of our long-patented rule. "3 weeks Del, 3 weeks." Oh, he knew how to press the right buttons.

* * *

The 3 Weeks Rule: If you have an upcoming decision to make you should ask yourself the following question: "When I look back on this decision in 3 weeks, will I regret deciding to go for it"? If the answer is yes, don't do it. You'd probably still be pretty damn pissed at yourself three weeks later for choosing to spontaneously quit your job, right?

But if the answer is no, then send it! 3 weeks from now will you *really* remember that extra hour of sleep? Or will you remember the beauty of that sunrise hike that you woke up early for instead? Something that is comfortable in the moment (an extra hour of sleep) pales in comparison to events with delayed gratification (a sunrise hike) when viewed with a "3 weeks" lens.

* * *

Back to the story: Was I tired? Sure. Could I have used a little sleep? You bet. But the 3 weeks rule, *my own self-enforced 3 weeks rule*, yielded one option and one option only. I had to go.

We left our house and drove 6 hours to the largest bluegrass festival in the country without tickets, parking passes, or an idea where we were going to sleep. The concert was sold out for months and the closest affordable sleeping arrangement was an hour away from Telluride.

Long story short we ended up having the greatest weekend of my life. A road trip that started with zero plans ended with us taking tequila shots with a Hollywood actress, receiving free $600 backstage passes from one of the bluegrass artists, and sleeping under the stars.

* * *

So back to the overall message here...that free yoga class in the park? Even though you've never done yoga? GO.

That volleyball Meetup group looking for one more player tonight? GO.

And of course, you better say yes to that spontaneous road trip that will certainly lead to a little less sleep but might just lead to laugh-so-hard-your-stomach-hurts memories 25 years from now.

You're not 50 with a family yet. Say yes to random, spontaneous things. I guarantee they'll lead to some of your favorite memories when you *are* 50...

HOW TO FLY LIKE A BO$$

I f consulting has taught me one thing, it is how to take advantage of the little tricks of the trade when it comes to traveling. Here are a few secrets (some more obvious than others) for how to travel like a pro.

AVOID CONNECTING IN SMALL AIRPORTS

I want to tell you to avoid connections all together, but I realize not everyone lives in a hub city and this isn't always feasible. Connections are terrible for two reasons: first, they take significantly longer than flying direct (add at least an hour and a half to two hours to your trip), and second, you run the risk of missing your connection. Small airports in particular are miserable because if you miss your connection there is a good chance there isn't another flight to your destination for that day. Unless you love spending cold winter nights in a Best Western attached to the Syracuse airport (no offense Jack) or driving from Columbus to Chicago (true story), I'd recommend flying direct or connecting in hub cities.

CLEAR COOKIES BEFORE BOOKING FLIGHTS

Airlines have the ability to track which flights you are looking at and increase prices based off your search history. This is true and yes, kind of terrifying. If you are hunting around for the best price and notice a flight go up in a matter of minutes, go to your internet settings and clear your cookies. This should return the flight to its normal price.

BUY FLIGHTS ON A TUESDAY

This one is self-explanatory, but flight prices fluctuate depending on the day of the week and are their lowest on a Tuesday. If prices are still high, Hopper is an app that analyzes billions of flights to tell you exactly when to purchase your ticket.

TAKE ADVANTAGE OF AIRLINE/HOTEL CREDIT CARDS

Maximize your points by signing up for an airline/hotel credit card during a promotion. The United MileagePlus Explorer Card typically offers 50,000 miles if you spend $3,000 in the first three months. This is enough points to get you a round trip flight to Australia (I know because I just booked one). Get two of the four Southwest credit cards and you get Companion Pass, which allows you to fly someone with you for *free* on any flight (as long as they are physically with you). Even better, this perk lasts for two calendar years. We could go on and on but the point is to look into credit cards that have airline-specific perks--some of them are too good to pass up.

NO ONE PAYS $250/NIGHT FOR A HOTEL ROOM

Have you ever traveled to a random city, Googled a close by hotel, and have your jaw drop when you saw the price? I have. I've seen hotel rooms in Oklahoma City go for $300/night. Who the hell pays for that? The answer is nobody. Hotel rooms are interesting because two people can book the same room on the same day and pay completely different prices. Every large company has negotiated rates with hotel chains that essentially cuts the price in half. When booking hotel stays, check with your company to see if they have a code for a negotiated rate. (Or if your company doesn't have one, a quick Google search for "XYZ Corporate Lodging Code" should do the trick).

TSA PRE-CHECK IS THE BEST $85 YOU'LL EVER SPEND

Period. It lasts 5 years and will save you hours of waiting in TSA lines. No one likes taking their shoes off & laptops out when going through security. Buy pre-check. And if you plan to leave the country even one time in the next 5 years, spend the extra $15 to tack Global Entry onto it (you'll breeze through customs).

ALWAYS CARRY YOUR LUGGAGE ON

The obvious reason to never check a bag is because it runs the risk of getting lost / smashed underneath the plane. The less obvious reason is carrying a bag on gives you flexibility. You can only get on a standby list if you do not have a checked bag.

AVOID LAGUARDIA LIKE THE PLAGUE

This NYC airport is great in concept; you can get cheap flights in and out of here, and it is close to Manhattan. What people don't tell you is if you fly into LaGuardia your flight will get delayed / cancelled. The sun will rise, you will pay taxes, and you will get delayed flying into LaGuardia. Oh and if by some miracle you aren't delayed, it's a quick 5 mile trip into Manhattan once you land, right? You'd be better off walking. It might be five miles but welcome to NYC traffic. It's a solid $60 hour-long cab ride into Manhattan after you land. Fly into JFK or Newark and save yourself the hassle.

DON'T PUT UP WITH SHITTY WINDOWS WHEN IT'S -10 DEGREES OUTSIDE

S etting: It's February of 2015 and Chicago is going through one of those "polar vortex" stints. You know, the kind of stint where the thermometer reads -10 and with windchill it's -20. Yeah, that cold.

Anyways, our Chicago apartment was *old as shit* and had windows that probably hadn't been replaced since it was built. I distinctly remember having to get up from the table to run my hands under hot water just so I could type on my laptop. Not only was our apartment freezing, but we were also hemorrhaging heat (and a hefty electricity bill) through our crumbling windows.

Pro tip: *you can, and should, negotiate with landlords.* If you are a current tenant, please understand the following: it takes a lot of time, effort, and money to replace you as a tenant. Landlords will do *a lot* to keep you in their apartment vs. finding someone else to pay rent. Once you understand this concept, the apartment world is your oyster. Also, understand that your negotiating power is never higher than the few months before your lease is about to end.

Before signing up for our second year, we had some *serious* stipulations. Each and every one of them was met, including receiving brand new windows in our living room, a brand new refrigerator, and a brand new stove.

Don't suffer through polar vortexes...learn to negotiate with landlords instead.

SUNDAY NIGHT MOVIE NIGHT (AND OTHER WEEKLY RITUALS)

In college, schedules are much more defined. In the real world, not so much. Even if you and all your friends have a typical "9 to 5 job" no job is actually 9 to 5. There are extended work obligations that might keep you in the office late, company outings, holiday dinners...and that's before we even get to your social obligations out of college--the weekend trips to visit people etc.

Before you know it, months can fly by without connecting with the friends you have in your actual place of living!

Establishing weekly or monthly routines (different than your morning routine) can provide you with some much needed consistency in your life.

For example, we've always had a "Sunday Night Movie Night" routine. It is nice to know that, no matter how crazy of a week/weekend it was, this routine would be there consistently. At 7:30pm on a Sunday, we would always know where to find our friends: on our couch ready to watch a movie and catch up on life.

Movie night is just one example. It could be a monthly "Supper Club" that you host potluck style on the first Thursday of every month. It could be a bi-weekly poker tournament on Tuesday nights. And technically it doesn't even have to involve friends! A weekly or monthly routine that is blocked off on your calendar can be extremely beneficial (Ex: A 30-minute "Weekly Planning" session for yourself blocked off at 5pm every Sunday).

The point is, routines can go beyond morning routines. Setting up some form of consistent routines in your life will give you a sense of calm in an otherwise hectic lifestyle.

DO MORE OF WHAT MAKES YOU HAPPY

The chapter title screams "Duh! Of course I should do that!" but on further inspection, it is truly incredible how few people in the world, particularly young 20-somethings, have any idea what truly makes them happy.

"Well going out with my friends and drinking a lot of beers is really fun and makes me happy, so I guess I'll just keep doing that!"

While we must admit, going out with friends and drinking a lot of beers *is* fun and *does* make us happy from time to time, we ask you to go one more additional step.

What makes you happy *all on your own, with no one around?*

You see, once in the real world, you deal with a lot of shit every day. These days there are so many external pressures out there, if you don't take control of your life, life will take control of you. This means if you don't actively seek what makes you happy all on your own, you'll end up doing what the rest of the world *thinks* you should do to be happy...and most of the time the rest of the world is simply wrong.

Too many people rely on others for their happiness (i.e. the guy that always has a girlfriend), and in turn never achieve happiness. The reason being is people are inherently selfish and when push comes to shove that best friend of yours will prioritize their own happiness over yours. Sometimes in order to be happy you have to be selfish. And that's okay! Nothing is more important than being happy.

WHAT MAKES ME HAPPY

What makes me happy, you ask? *Identifying the task at hand and applying 100% of my focus to it.* That's what makes me happy. It could be something as tedious as *doing laundry while only thinking about doing laundry.* This exclusive mental state is what I've figured out leads to my happiness and is something I seek out whenever I feel out of sorts.

Pretty weird, right? I would agree. And yours will likely be different. But the important thing here is to *actively figure out what makes you happy...and then do it when needed!*

* * *

I'll leave you with three simple steps to achieve happiness:
1. Identify that you are unhappy (which can be the hardest step).
2. Determine what will make you happy and make this your highest priority.
3. Do it!

5:20

This is the most important chapter of this book.

If you take one thing away from this book it is this: *live every day to the fullest, and appreciate every day like it's your last.*

Life happens fast. One day you are learning how to ice skate by pushing a cone around, you blink and you're taking those awkward side-by-side photos before senior prom. You blink again and you're shaking the dean's hand at college graduation. Then the real world happens and time goes even faster; people start getting married, buying houses, and having kids. You'll have a moment in the next few years where you're at your childhood best friend's wedding and think "Holy shit, I remember playing baseball in the cul de sac with him like it was yesterday. Where did the time go?"

Most adults put their lives on autopilot and float through their days. They wake up at the same time each day, sit in their cubes for 8 hours, leave at exactly 5:01 PM, make dinner, watch Netflix, and go to bed. They repeat this routine Monday through Friday for the next 40 years; never taking a risk and always pointing at retirement as the time to start "living their lives." The problem is once they reach retirement they are old, tired, and unhealthy from sitting at a desk. They lose the motivation to travel the world or visit every ballpark in America like they talked about years ago. If you visit a senior living home and ask the residents a piece of advice, you will hear this same message: appreciate the moment more!

Why do people need to become old to realize how valuable life is? Why doesn't everyone recognize that every day is a gift?

In my opinion, people subconsciously put their lives on autopilot for two reasons:

1. **It is easier**
2. **People are always looking forward to the next thing**

Let's dissect each of these a bit further.

IT'S EASIER

People are creatures of habit. So much so that they repeat the same actions day after day even when their actions do not increase their happiness. Routine is healthy, but being complacent with an "average" day is not.

You should wake up every day and think, "How can I make this the best day possible?"

I'm not saying quit your job and go skydiving. *I'm saying break free of the "average" day mindset and think how you can make that Tuesday feel like a Saturday.* Little things can make a day go from a 4/10 to a 10/10. It is important to *know what makes you happy and go do it* (See Chapter "Do More of What Makes You Happy"). A lot of times, making yourself happy is not convenient and requires more effort/time than you think you have. Do it anyways. Your happiness should be your highest priority.

Never settle with having an average day. Life is too short. Do the little things that you know make you happy. Wear those fun socks to work, buy that expensive steak dinner, reward yourself with a new phone. You are worth it.

THE NEXT THING

"I will be happy when..." and "I'll be happy if..." are the most toxic statements in the English language. You can fill in the blank with "get promoted", "make six figures", or "fall in love" to name a few. The reason why so many people cannot live in the moment is because they are always chasing the future. And guess what? They will never catch it. As soon as they get that promotion, they will immediately start looking towards the next. One of the best pieces of career advice I've received was to enjoy my current role because each phase comes with new challenges.

I would like to take this one step further: Do not only enjoy every phase of your career, but enjoy every phase of your life. The best way we have found to appreciate life is to set time aside each day to reflect on the beauty of that day- this is what we call our 5:20.

* * *

THE ORIGIN OF 5:20 (AS TOLD BY JACK)

The date was November 5, 2012 and I was on an abroad program called *Semester at Sea*. In short, we traveled the world with 500 other college students and "studied" along the way. To say it was a life-changing experience is an understatement.

But I digress. On November 5, 2012 I looked at my calendar and could not believe what I saw. *We only had one month left.* The voyage was scheduled to finish on December 5 and I could not believe how time had flown by.

And so, right then and there, I made a vow:

I would appreciate & truly soak in *each and every day* of the remaining month. I would acknowledge when another day had come and gone by having a moment, even if only a brief, fleeting moment, to simply take a deep breath, smile, and *live completely in the present.*

I have done this every single day since, spanning over six years...and don't plan on stopping.

OKAY, SO WHAT IS 5:20 EXACTLY?

5:20 happens to be my time of the day to truly appreciate the moment. At the time, I chose 5:20 because it was right after classes ended on the ship, but *you can choose any time of the day that works best for you.* Or, perhaps you prefer to choose an *event* over a time, such as passing the same corner on your daily walk to work.

How to implement 5:20 in your daily life
Okay, you've chosen your time (or event) that works best with your schedule. Now, you really have two steps remaining:
1. **Set an alarm** on your watch or phone for that time every day.
2. **When the alarm goes off,** no matter where you are, or what you are doing, take a moment, even if only one or two seconds, to stop doing whatever you are doing, take one deep breath, and truly, **deeply appreciate the moment you are in.**

WHAT YOU'LL START TO FIND

At the beginning, you'll find this exercise awkward. But if you stick with it, here's what will happen: you will start to look forward to your 5:20 moments. It will be your way to completely separate from the world, look within, and appreciate the simple fact that you are alive...while at the same time acknowledge that another day of your finite life has passed. Instead of viewing this in a negative light, be thankful for the day you just had!

We said it at the beginning of the chapter and we will finish with it: there is no more important chapter of this entire book. *If you take one single lesson out of this book to actually implement in your life, make it this one.* You won't be disappointed.

EPILOGUE

They say a picture is worth a thousand words. Thanks to everyone who has been a part of these formative years.

–Joey & Jack

JOEY & JACK

Jerry's Wedding, College Boys, Colorado Fly Fishing, Red Rocks

JACK & TUCKER

Backyard Snowboarding, All–Delehey Attack Line, Delehey Kids, Nantucket

WE WERE FRESH OUT OF COLLEGE ONCE TOO

Celtics/Cavs, Corporate Life, Friendsgiving 2015, Work Snack, Kenny 2.0, Last day in Chicago, Gasparilla 2016, Tailgating, Narrows Hike

WE WERE FRESH OUT OF COLLEGE ONCE TOO (CONT.)

#FreeBrady @ NFL Draft, Ragnar 2016, SantaCon 2016, Surfing in LA, Telluride (Road Trip Story), The Boys in Chicago, Tough Mudder, New Years 2016, Blow Drying our Windows in –10 degree weather (see, we really weren't making this up)

Made in the USA
Middletown, DE
28 January 2019